Vegan Ket‹

The Ultimate Ketog
Cookbook, With Low-Carb and
Vegan Keto Bread Recipes to
Maximize Weight Loss and Special
Ideas to Build Your Keto Vegan
Meal Plan

By Tyler Allen

Summary

Chapter 1: What Is Ketogenic Diet and How Does it Work?

The ketogenic diet is one of the most popular diets today, with many celebrity endorsements, social media attention, and ongoing scientific research to support the benefits of eating keto. Traditionally, diets center around low calories and reducing fat, whereas the keto way of eating works by increasing the amount of healthy fats and reducing carbohydrates. This has the effect of switching the body's main source of fuel from glucose and carbohydrates to stored fat, which produces significant results in a short period of time. Initially, the ketogenic diet appears to be another fad, though historically, it was developed nearly one hundred years ago for the treatment of certain medical conditions, including epilepsy (specifically reducing seizures), regulating insulin, and other health benefits. There were positive results for both children and adults alike—significant reduction or elimination of epileptic seizures and improved cognitive abilities. Weight loss was another benefit of the diet because of the low-carbohydrate intake, which is one of the major reasons that the ketogenic diet grew in popularity. As medications were developed, this way of eating became less common until just recently, with a new surge of health and diet consciousness.

Most people's diets consist of a high level of carbohydrates: bread, pasta, grains, pastries, and sugary foods. These food items are offered at every restaurant, drive-through, and coffee shop, so they are generally difficult to avoid. The ketogenic way of eating aims to reduce the level of carbohydrates in our diets for 100+ grams per day to a mere 20 grams at the maximum. Healthy fats (monounsaturated and polyunsaturated fats) from natural oils and foods are the largest part of the keto diet at 70-75%, followed by protein at 20%, and carbohydrates, making up the remaining 0-5%:

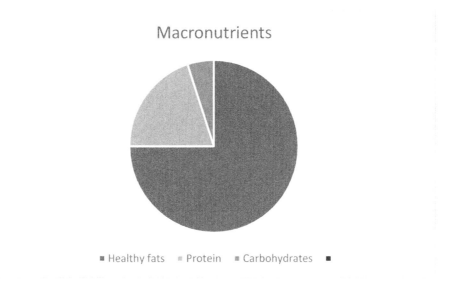

How Does Keto Work?

When your body burns fuel, the first source is always carbohydrates and glucose. With a typical high-carb diet, these are readily available and provide a lot of energy. If the amount of carbohydrates in your diet is high, your body will continue to access this source as fuel, moving to fat stores as the next option, only once the carbs are completely depleted. When carbs are significantly reduced in your meal plan, your body will shift to fat stores. At this point, carbohydrates and glucose are low and used up quickly.

What Keto Is and Isn't

Keto isn't a new concept, nor it is a temporary trend; it is a sustainable, long-term solution for the prevention and treatment of many health conditions, as well as weight loss goals. As with every diet, there have been divisive opinions and reactions to the low-carb way of eating, from adverse health effects to gaining back all of the weight that was lost if carbs are added back into the diet. There are a lot of misconceptions about the keto diet, which can easily be cleared up with a bit of research and reading about the history and studies conducted on this diet:

What keto is	What keto is not
A sustainable, long-term diet for weight loss and maintenance, prevention, and treatment of certain medical conditions	It's trendy and popular, though not just a "fad" diet
Supported by scientific research and studies from nearly 100 years ago	Unhealthy. Although the keto diet is not for everyone and may have restrictions depending on your individual medical condition(s), it is relatively safe for most people
A nutritious, balanced diet consisting of natural and healthy fats and moderate amounts of protein, with nutrients, fiber, and a small amount of carbohydrates	Overly restrictive. The low-carb diet may appear challenging, though there are delicious options to replace high-carb foods with healthy, nutritious meals
Flexible, easy to follow, and can fit within your budget	It's an expensive diet. It can be a challenge to find the right foods, though, with some effort and budgeting, it can cost the same as any diet.

Ketosis and Ketones

Ketosis is the process by which your body becomes adapted to fat, switching to fat as the fuel-burning source. This occurs when ketones are produced by the liver, as a response to low-carb consumption. During the state, you may experience some changes in your body, such as high energy and better mental focus. During your first experience of ketosis, you may experience "keto flu" symptoms, which include fatigue, light nausea, and other flu-like symptoms, though these are temporary and will disappear within the first two weeks. The long-term benefits of the ketogenic diet outweigh the initial side effects, especially adapting to a vegan ketogenic diet, which combines the health benefits of both ways of eating into a sustainable, healthy diet.

Once your body becomes accustomed to ketosis, you'll begin to notice weight loss, high levels of energy, and other benefits. Blood sugar levels will drop as insulin becomes regulated better. Cravings for sugary and processed foods will drop drastically. If weight loss is a goal, you will notice a significant change within weeks or one to two months.

What Is the Science Behind Ketosis and Producing Ketones?

Ketones are produced by the body in response to low glucose levels. This occurs when all carbohydrates and glucose is used up for fuel. The level of insulin will fall, and a process of beta-oxidation begins. Beta-oxidation occurs when fatty acids move from fat cells and into the body's bloodstream, which results in the production of ketones. There are three different types of ketones that become present in the blood once ketosis is reached and maintained. The first ketone created is acetoacetate (AcAc), in the initial state of ketosis, followed by the production of two more types: BHB (B-hydroxybutyrate) and acetone. Acetone is produced less than BHB, as more of a by-product of AcAc, and discarded by the body. When a state of ketosis is maintained, your body will be fat-adapted and continue to burn fat stores instead of glucose. In order to remain in this state and continue to benefit from rapid weight loss, a low carbohydrate level of under 20 grams per day is required. In order to achieve a nutritious state of ketosis, it is important to track macronutrients and make healthy food choices. This book will provide food options, meal plans, and recipes as tools for your new way of eating.

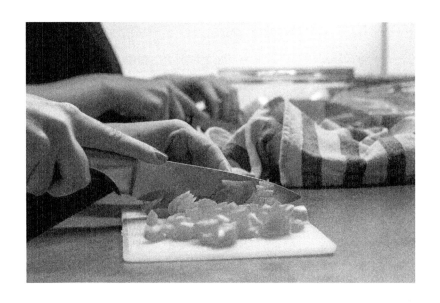

Chapter 2: What Is a Vegan Diet?

The vegan diet is a plant-based diet without any meat products or by-products like dairy, eggs, or any foods that contain ingredients derived from animals. Veganism or plant-based eating is, and continues to remain, a popular and sustainable way of eating for people all over the world, for a variety of reasons: religious, environmental, ethical, or for better health. It is a beneficial way of eating, as it reduces many conditions caused by animal products, such as high cholesterol, heart disease, cardiovascular problems, and weight gain.

A plant-based diet contains much more variety and taste than many people think. When your diet is centered around meat, vegetables become the side portions or options, as opposed to being the main feature. There are plenty of exotic and interesting vegetables and fruits, even local foods, which can be explored and added to meals. Dairy products, such as milk, eggs, and butter, can be easily substituted by non-dairy products that are coconut or almond-based. Tempeh and miso, fermented soy, as well as firm tofu, are often used instead of eggs or meat products in vegan meals.

Why Is Vegan Diet Healthy?

It is lower in calories, trans, and saturated fats (found in animal products), and plant-based foods are less processed and tend to be more natural than dairy and meat. As with any diet, there are advantages and disadvantages to the vegan diet, which will be explored later in this book. Overall, vegan or plant-based eating is sustainable and healthy, as long as you meet all of your dietary and nutrient requirements. A vegan diet is best to begin in stages, first by eliminating some meats (usually red meats), followed by poultry, fish, eggs, and dairy. Vegetarian is a good option for some people who wish to keep dairy and eggs in their diet either in the short term or long term. It can be a "gateway" to veganism from a meat-centric diet. The pace and mean by which you progress from your current way of eating to a plant-based diet should be an individual plan that fits within your lifestyle, taking into consideration any medical or health needs.

The different stages of vegetarianism are divided into the following categories:

Semi-vegetarian: This is not actually vegetarian, though it limits the types of meat in your diet. Most people who follow this way of eating eliminate or strictly limit red meats, such as beef and pork, eating mostly poultry and seafood. This diet usually includes eggs and dairy.

Pescatarian: the only meat consumed in this diet is fish, which is a step further from semi-vegetarian. Some people choose this diet in the long term, and they even incorporate the pescatarian diet with keto, as fish contains a lot of healthy fats and protein beneficial in a low-carb diet. This way of eating can also bridge a transition to veganism.

Lacto-vegetarian: This form of vegetarianism restricts all meat and egg products, although it includes dairy. Yogurt, cheese, milk, and butter are usually a part of this diet.

Ovo-vegetarian: Eggs are the only animal products included in this diet.

Lacto-ovo Vegetarian: As the name suggests, this combines the lacto and ovo types of vegetarian diet, which includes all dairy products and eggs while omitting all meat products.

While many people follow different variations of the vegetarian diet, sometimes, in combination with a low-carb diet or ketogenic diet, it can be either a long-term goal or a way to become more accommodated to a diet that is less reliant on meat products and processed food. In many variations of the keto diet, high levels of fats are often sourced from meats and dairy, which can still provide all of the benefits of keto eating. If you choose to incorporate both keto and vegan diets together, begin by reducing the number of animal products and decide which level you prefer (either one of the above vegetarian diets or progress to vegan).

Veganism: This form of vegetarianism differs from all other options for one reason—it is completely animal-free and plant-based. While it may take time to become comfortable with avoiding meat products, it is a process that should be done gently and carefully to ensure there are no nutrient deficiencies. It is the first goal of adapting to a vegan keto diet before reducing carbs and adding healthy, vegan fats to adjust for a long-term way of healthy eating and lifestyle.

Chapter 3: The Vegan Keto Diet: Why Is it the Most Beneficial Way to Eat?

The vegan and ketogenic diets both provide a lot of benefits on their own, and in combination, the impact on your health and weight loss are tremendous. On their own, both diets have specific characteristics, as indicated in the following chart. While both diets may seem completely opposite, they are both balanced and sustainable ways of eating:

Characteristics of the Keto Diet	Characteristics of the Vegan Diet
Low in carbohydrates and sugars	Plant-based. No animal products or by-products
Whole foods, as much as possible. Processed and packaged food items are avoided. Meat and dairy are included.	Whole foods, as much as possible. Processed and packaged food items are avoided.
Promotes the body's ability to switch from burning glucose and carbs to stored fats, resulting in weight loss	Vegan foods tend to be lower in calories and trans fats, making them easier to digest and metabolize

How does combining both vegan and ketogenic diet help you optimize your health and help you lose weight? When you factor in the low-carb intake of the keto diet, plus the high fiber and moderate-to-low caloric volume of plant-based foods, it draws the best of both diets into one powerful eating lifestyle. One of the major ways in which the ketogenic diet is successful in promoting a state of ketosis, which effectively produces ketones in your body to further break down fat instead of glucose as the primary source of fuel.

Vegan Ketosis: How Does Ketosis Work While on a Vegan Diet?

Achieving ketosis while on the vegan keto diet is like the regular ketogenic plan, only without the meat products. How is vegan ketosis different? First, as with regular keto, you'll need to increase your intake of healthy fats while eliminating sugar and carbs, as much as possible. A lot of fats can be found in animal products, and these are often used to increase fat content (eggs, milk, meat, oils), which can make it a challenge to find vegan alternatives. By nature, most meat alternatives are lower in fats and, therefore, do not produce as much energy for the fat-adapted body. This can be easily remedied with a bit of research and finding quality stores with the right food products. Coconut oil, seeds (hemp hearts, flaxseeds), nuts (specifically macadamia nuts), MCT oil, olive oil, avocados, and avocado oil are among the top choices for vegan fats. They are excellent sources of fatty acids and omega 3, and they can supplement your fuel, where plant-based options may seem limited.

Vegan Ketosis: How Is it Different From Regular Ketosis?

Ketosis is basically the same, whether you follow a regular ketogenic diet (including meat and dairy products) or a vegan keto plan. There may be some differences in the initial stages of ketosis, such as experiencing the keto "flu," which is characterized by temporary symptoms of fatigue, loss of focus and energy, and sometimes, nausea within the first two weeks. If your body is already adapted to a vegan diet, and you are strictly on this diet, these initial symptoms may manifest less and can be avoidable. This is because of the way plant-based foods are easily digested and your body may already be adapted to less carbohydrates, especially if you avoid processed foods (including packaged vegan foods). The major difference of regular ketosis versus vegan ketosis is in the level of fat you need to consume to reach and maintain the production of ketones, although overall, the experience and results are essentially the same.

The Advantages and Disadvantages of the Vegan Keto Diet

As with any diet, there are always considerations to make, concerning present health, life circumstances, and medical conditions. If you are experiencing a lot of stress or a major life event, it's best to make a slow transition or postpone any major dietary changes, even improvements. A diet that benefits your body includes your mind and well-being, and all components of your life should be weighed carefully. Generally, the vegan keto diet is beneficial for many reasons, and there are some characteristics or traits that may be considered less desirable or disadvantageous, depending on your expectations.

Advantages of the Vegan Keto Diet	Disadvantages of the Vegan Keto Diet
Diminishes the probability of developing certain types cancer, diabetes (type 2), and heart disease	Limits the amount of healthy fats due to no inclusion of meat, eggs, or dairy
Significantly lowers your chances of developing high blood pressure and related conditions	Plant-based fats are available, though may be expensive or hard to find in some regions or stores, depending on where you live.

Reduction of "bad" LDL cholesterol and improving good cholesterol	It requires effort to track and include all daily nutrients to ensure you are not deficient. Nutrient deficiencies can be avoided on a vegan keto diet, though it can easily occur when specific nutrients are missing (vitamin D, B12, for example).
Significant weight loss and higher levels of energy and mood stability	Lack of fresh, natural plant-based foods in some regions can make this diet challenging to follow.

Chapter 4: Getting Started on the Vegan Keto Diet: Is it Right for You?

How do you know if the vegan keto lifestyle is for you? There are many factors to consider before you begin to ensure this way of eating is right for you. These include medical conditions, your lifestyle, dietary restrictions, and goals, as well as your commitment to achieving good health and weight loss. Considering how you eat currently is a good first step in determining how to proceed. For example, if you already adhere to a vegetarian or vegan diet, it will be much easier to gradually reduce carbohydrates in your diet until you reach the ketogenic level of up to 20 grams of carbs per day. On the other hand, if you are already following a ketogenic diet and looking to eliminate meat and dairy products, this will be a gradual process of eliminating one or several animal foods at a time until your diet is plant-based, while you keep a low-carb intake.

Before You Begin the Vegan Keto Diet: Steps to Take

What are the first steps? This depends on the status of your current diet and lifestyle and how well you can adjust and adapt to a new way of eating. While it is best to consult a medical professional about the impact of changing your diet on any specific health conditions, switching to a vegan keto diet is one of the best investments in your health for prevention against disease and improving health overall:

Step 1: How do you eat currently? Does your meal plan consist of careful planning, preparation, and budgeting, or do you often eat "on the go" with little time for consideration? If you have a busy life, simple and easy meals that can be prepared quickly or the night before are best for you. Keep this in mind when choosing recipes compatible with plant-based keto meals. Find some time to prepare meals for the week when it's convenient, such as on a Sunday evening before a workweek or another suitable time. Meal planning for a week will reduce a lot of stress and effort during busier days when there more things to juggle and coordinate.

Step 2: What does your grocery list look like? Do you stick with a list or buy compulsively? Buying impulsively or sporadically is fun sometimes, especially when you want to try a new recipe or food choice, though most, if not all, shopping is best planned with a list. This will keep you on track with cost, time, and making good food decisions. Examine your current list, if you have one: are most of the foods plant-based, low-carb, fresh, or processed and packaged? Is the list a combination of different foods or fairly rigid, centering around a limited number of foods or products?

Step 3: Where do you shop? Local and organic produce and food is the best option, though not always affordable or available, depending on where you live. If you have the option of shopping for local produce at farmer's markets and small, family-owned businesses, this will only support the local economy, and it will likely help your budget and improve the quality of food you eat. For baking supplies, try shopping in bulk or at stores that offer bulk as an option, as this will minimize packaging and keep portions and costs related to your food plan appropriate and relevant.

Step 4: What should be on your list? Once you decide that the vegan diet is right for you, it's time to work on a shopping list! When you review the list of foods appropriate for both ketogenic and vegan eating, you can search for effective alternatives to some (or all) of your foods to find out where they can be purchased, the costs, and when they are in season.

The First Week of Your Vegan Keto Diet

If you are planning on major results, this is one of the best ways to eat. Starting gradually by replacing one or two major items per week until your weekly grocery list is keto and plant-based is highly doable. Or, you can begin an overhaul with a fresh new list of vegan and keto-friendly foods. The second option may feel like more of a shock, and this may work for some people looking for drastic results within a relatively short period of time. The best approach for diving into this diet is a two-step process: adapting to plant-based eating and then reducing carbs.

Adapting to a Plant-Based Diet

Going vegan is a big change, especially if you enjoy meat, eggs, and dairy as a part of your diet. Replacing animal products with plant-based alternatives can be done gradually or quickly, depending on what pace works best for you. For example, start by eliminating red meats from your diet (pork, beef, etc.), and either replace them with poultry and fish or with a vegetarian substitute. Try this for one to two weeks before replacing all meat, including seafood and poultry, with plant-based options. At this stage, don't worry about lowering carbs, though you can try choosing soy and plant-based burgers and meat alternatives, instead of increasing the portion of rice, bread, or pasta you may currently enjoy. When in doubt, substitute a meat item with a vegetable option.

As you become adjusted to a meat-free diet, begin substituting the milk, yogurt, butter, and cheese items next. This may be as easy as cutting them out altogether or looking for a plant-based product. If you opt for a vegan cheese or butter substitute, read the ingredients carefully because even soy or vegetable alternatives can be loaded with extra salt, hidden sugars, and additives. Coconut oil and olive oil are excellent choices for baking and cooking instead of butter or margarine. Cultured yogurt, unsweetened, can replace the dairy version. Instead of flavoring food with cheese, try different herbs, spices, and grilled vegetables. This can work wonders for vegetarian burgers and casseroles.

It may take a while to switch your meat and dairy foods for vegan options, and for this reason, give yourself time. Changing too quickly may trigger cravings and switching back and forth or "cheating" on your diet. Plan ahead, take it slow, and try a new plant-based food before deciding whether to include them in your diet. If tofu or soy products sound unappealing to you, consider the various forms and ways soy can be prepared and enjoyed. Smoked tofu, pan-seared curried tempeh, and miso soup are all delicious variations that may change your outlook on soy foods and their limitless possibilities.

Going Vegan: Reducing Carbohydrates

Once a plant-based plan is established and you become comfortable with a regular plan, it's time to focus on reducing carbohydrates. Review your current shopping list or items you enjoy as part of a plant-based diet and determine the following:

- Do you include a lot of packaged and processed vegan foods in your diet? This may include energy bars, powders, dried fruit, and salty snacks.

- Check the sugar and glucose ingredients and levels in your diet. This includes fruits, preservatives (jams, condiments, etc.), and both natural and artificial sweeteners.
- Bread, pasta, grains, and rice: are these items included in your weekly shopping?
- Do you snack often and does this include chips, candies, and soft drinks?

All these items above are high in carbohydrates and should be either eliminated or strictly reduced. This can be done over a comfortable pace so that your body becomes used to smaller changes, instead of a complete overnight overhaul. Here are a few examples that will help get you started:

- Switch a bag of chips for almonds, walnuts, or peanuts. If you have a nut allergy, try dried coconut or fresh berries as a snack
- Replace soda, fruit juice, and other sugary drinks with regular water, sparkling water, or naturally unsweetened iced tea. Coffee is acceptable, without any added sugar, flavors, or preservatives. In some grocery stores, natural sodas with low or zero carb sweeteners are available and taste just like regular soda.
- One of the most challenging aspects of the keto diet is avoiding pasta and bread products. Baked goods are a staple in many diets. Grains and beans are also the main

sources of nutrients in many diets and also high in carbohydrates. Instead of getting rid of all of these items at once, work on reducing or removing one item at a time. There are vegan keto baked goods that can be easily prepared with simple ingredients. Vegetables and salads can take the place of grains, rice, and pasta.

- Take an inventory of the fresh and frozen fruits and vegetables in your diet. Begin to reduce carbs in this area by eliminating high-starch (and high-glucose) foods first, such as potatoes, peas, carrots, and bananas. Add or increase dark green vegetables, green beans, turnips, green peppers, berries, avocados, and coconut milk (unsweetened). Occasionally, small amounts of citrus fruit and rhubarb are acceptable.

It will take time to adjust your diet, and the results will be worth it. One of the greatest advantages of adapting to a vegan keto diet is the amount of knowledge you gain from learning about the nutritious value of foods. This experience will help encourage better and more thoughtful choices during your trips to the grocery store or local market.

Chapter 5: What Foods Can You Eat on the Vegan Keto Diet?

Choosing Low-Carb, Plant-Based Foods to Meet Your Diet goals

Choosing the right vegan and ketogenic foods and keeping those choices consistent are the keys to success on this diet. Keep foods as natural and simple as possible, and build your diet and shopping list around these items.

Soy

Tofu, tempeh, and miso are all forms of soy. If you have an allergic reaction to soybeans and soy products, it may be beneficial to switch to fermented soy foods, such as miso and tempeh, which are usually more tolerable. Soy is considered a "superfood," as it contains most, if not all, required daily nutrients: protein, fiber, calcium, and vitamins. Some soy products are fortified with vitamin D and other nutrients. Fermented soy products contain B12, which is usually considered exclusive to meat and some dairy products.

One of the most versatile foods and a staple in many countries and regions around the world, soy can be incorporated into any meal of the day, including dessert and snacks. Complete meals and food preparation techniques are centered around soy, which makes it a primary source of a vegan diet. Some prepared soy products may contain additives and marinades with sweeteners that contribute to an increase in carbohydrates. The best option for soy is natural, unsweetened, and unflavored tofu and tempeh products. This includes soy milk, yogurts, and other soy or dairy substitutes. Avoid any items with added flavors (natural or unnatural), as they will increase glucose levels.

Seeds and Nuts

Almonds, walnuts, pumpkin seeds, peanuts, flaxseeds, and hemp hearts are all low in carb content and highly nutritious options for a vegan keto diet. Pumpkin seeds are high in protein, magnesium, iron, and zinc. Just a handful a day as a snack can provide a significant amount of your daily needs. Hemp seeds contain healthy fats that work well to increase the overall amount of fats you need to maintain ketosis. These seeds also contain protein and have been known to reduce blood pressure and provide energy. Sunflower seeds contain amino acids and protein, similar to pumpkin seeds; they can be added as a snack to your diet in between meals.

Chia Seeds

These amazing seeds deserve a category of their own because of its numerous benefits and usability in many meals, drinks, and supplements. Originating from South America, chia seeds are high in protein, amino acids, fiber, and vitamins. They have grown in popularity in many diets, including paleo, ketogenic, and vegan diets. Smoothies, baked goods, salads, and desserts are just a few options where chia seeds can be added. Mixed with other forms of protein such as seeds or soy to create puddings and smoothies or as a topping to a salad or main meal, chia seeds are easy to find and available in most grocery stores. They are usually found in bulk stores, where they are less expensive and may be available in several varieties.

Mushrooms

Shiitake, portobello, and other varieties of mushrooms can be enjoyed on a vegan keto diet.

Dark, Green Leafy Vegetables

One of the best features of the vegan keto diet is the number of vegetable options that are low in carbohydrates. When considering all low-carb options, green leafy vegetables are the most beneficial. These include kale, spinach, and arugula. Parsley, cilantro, dill, and many others can fit this category as well. Don't let the bitterness and unfamiliarity of kale deter you from trying them. There are plenty of recipes that enhance and change the flavor of these dark greens with various spices and oils. A simple example is baked kale chips, which are easy to prepare with a few ingredients. This is featured in the recipe section of this book. Spinach is a great addition to tofu scramble, skillet meals, and salads.

Cruciferous Vegetables: Cauliflower and Broccoli

These vegetables include cauliflower and broccoli, both of which are high in fiber.

Zucchini

This vegetable gets a special mention because it can be altered to replace some high-carb ingredients found in pasta dishes. Sliced, thin zucchini can make a great "noodle" for a lasagne, while spiral-sliced zucchini can replace noodles in soups or spaghetti or as a way to dress up a salad.

Fruits: Avocados, Berries, and on Occasion, Citrus Fruits

In the order that they are listed, enjoy avocado often; enjoy berries sometimes and citrus fruits on occasion. Avocado contains the least amount of carbohydrates of all fruits and can be enjoyed daily, as the carb content is very low. Berries have a low glycaemic level and can be added in small amounts to coconut milk as a treat or on their own as a snack. All berries are included: blackberries, strawberries, raspberries, and blueberries. Citrus fruits are more moderate in carbs, although they can be enjoyed in small doses. A splash of freshly squeezed lemon or lime in carbonated water or any recipe would be good. Rhubarb, though not often available and seasonal, is another low-to-moderate carb fruit that can be enjoyed in moderation.

Avocado

In addition to listing avocado with the fruit options, it is a valuable source of nutrients that can play a major role in your diet.

MCT and Coconut Oil

Coconut oil is readily available in most food stores, and MCT oil, the fat extract of coconut oil, is an excellent way to supplement the healthy fats in a vegan keto diet.

Low-Carb Sweeteners

These may seem too good to be real, as they taste like sugar while remaining completely carb-free or low-carb. Monk fruit is the best option and the most sugar-like in taste and texture. Other options include stevia and erythritol. Xylitol is another low-carb sweetener, though can be dangerous for pets, and should be avoided if you have a pet. Overall, all low-carb sweeteners are safe and can be found combined for maximum sweetness and taste.

Fermented Food Options

Tempeh and miso are fermented soy options, and other fermented foods are similarly keto and vegan-friendly, with many nutrients. Sauerkraut and kimchi are two main options that can be added as a side dish or snack. They both have a strong flavor and may be considered an acquired taste, though they can be enjoyed in small portions, along with a curried tofu dish or as a side with a soup or salad.

Seaweed and Sea Vegetables

Kelp, seaweed, and other sea-based vegetables are an excellent source of calcium, protein, and fiber. Seaweed is the most popular, usually found in sushi dishes. It can also be enjoyed as a ready-made snack in dried form.

How to Choose Foods and Balance Your Nutritional Needs

When you create your first shopping list, keep in mind your nutritional needs. For example, if you are active and want to build muscle by weight training, increasing the variety and level of protein could be a specific goal to keep in mind when choosing food. Maintain a regular metabolism, which means adding lots of fresh foods, natural produce, and a lot of fiber as major components of your diet.

Vegan Keto Bread: How to Make it and Add Into Your Regular Meals

Traditionally, baked goods, such as bread, pastries, and cakes are full of sugar and carbohydrates, which automatically eliminates them as options for a vegan keto diet. Fortunately, there are alternative ingredients that can be creatively used to recreate vegan and ketogenic versions of many baked foods to satisfy your craving. Before you consider baking the vegan keto way, create a simple and practical pantry of plant-based and ketogenic ingredients for your baking creations:

- **Low-carb sweeteners**. Monk fruit, stevia, and various other low-carb sweeteners can be found in dried granules like sugar and kept in a sealed container for a long time.

- **Almond and coconut flour**. Almond flour tends to be more costly and can often be combined with coconut flour in many recipes. It's also available in bulk. Coconut flour is drier and combines well with almond. Both options are best to have on hand, as they can be used separately or together in a variety of recipes.
- **Baking powder and baking soda**
- **Psyllium husk powder**
- **Vinegar**. Depending on the varieties of foods you enjoy and the recipes you create, vinegar tends to be low in carb content and can be safely added to many dishes
- **Oil**. Olive, avocado, and coconut oil are the best options
- **Nut butter**. Almond and peanut butter are the most popular options. Sesame seed butter is sometimes overlooked, although it's a protein-rich option that can easily replace other types of nut butter. Hazelnut butter is another option.
- **Coconut milk and cream**. These are invaluable ingredients for many dishes, from cakes to curries and puddings. They are available in cartons or cans.
- **Nutritional yeast**. This is good if you plan on baking vegan keto bread.
- **Psyllium husk** is a good ingredient to have, as it can effectively replace gluten in baking. It's good for your metabolism, high in fiber, and helps thicken or act as a

"glue" that keeps baked goods together. Psyllium can be bought in powder form and sometimes available in bulk, usually in natural food stores (or online).

- **Flaxseeds, chia seeds, and hemp hearts**. These may be optional or integral ingredients in a lot of recipes and a good boost of nutrients with any meal.

These ingredients create a strong foundation for many basic vegan keto baking recipes, which can be further expanded to include extracts, seeds, dried coconut flakes, and other low-carb options. There are many powders and supplements available in the market, specifically in natural and bulk foods stores. However, it's best to read the ingredients thoroughly to rule out additive and other items that add glucose or carbs. Keep ingredients as natural and as simple as possible. One brand of coconut flour should be the same as another, though watch for unusual or too many ingredients. Coconut milk can be sweetened or enhanced with additives, and for this reason, only unsweetened, pure versions of this milk should be included.

Vegan Keto Bread Recipe

Creating a vegan keto bread is not as difficult as it seems, though it may require a few "practice runs" to find the right recipe for your taste. Some breads can either be too hard or crumbly, and others lack the texture. In this section, three bread recipes are provided with their unique characteristics and flavors.

Flour-Free Almond Bread

This is a simple recipe that can be a good way to get acquainted with keto (and vegan) baking. It is best to begin with an easy recipe that doesn't require too much preparation or too many ingredients. This bread requires just three basic ingredients. It's gluten-free and can be supplemented with a dash of flaxseeds or hemp hearts for an additional boost of nutrients. Salt is also another option, depending on your preference. The main ingredients are as follows.

- 2 teaspoons psyllium husk powder
- 2 teaspoons of baking powder
- Olive or coconut oil (1-2 teaspoons)
- 1 ½ cups almond meal
- ½ cup of water

You need to add optional ingredients, as well as water, to make this recipe work. Almond meal is used instead of almond flour, as the almond meal retains the outer skin or shell of the almonds, while the flour doesn't (the skins are needed in this recipe). Keep some extra water on hand, just in case the dough needs a bit more. The water, when combined with the psyllium husk powder, will create a gel consistency, creating an effective egg replacement. Preheat the oven to 350 degrees. Spray some coconut oil or olive oil on a baking sheet and set aside. Mix the almond meal and baking powder in a medium-sized bowl. Combine the psyllium husk powder and water in another bowl, smaller in size. Stir the mixture for approximately 8 minutes to make a gel. Combine with the almond meal and baking powder and whisk all ingredients until thoroughly blended. Divide the mixture into 7-8 small muffin-like patties and bake in the oven for 25 minutes. For an easier bake, these can be prepared in a muffin sheet or shaped by hand and baked. Serve warm or cold. These can be toasted and used like regular bread.

Vegan Keto Seed Bread

This bread contains nuts and seeds and holds well together, unlike a lot of bread recipes that do not contain eggs. Psyllium husk powder is a good egg replacement, and for this reason, consider using this option with all bread and baking recipes where eggs would normally be used. There are considerably more ingredients in this bread than the first recipe, though the amounts are small and can be easily found and combined.

- 1 cup of water
- ½ cup hazelnuts
- ½ cup slivered or raw almonds
- ½ cup sesame seeds
- ½ cup pumpkin seeds
- ½ cup sunflower seeds
- ¼ cup chia seeds (any variety)
- 3 tablespoons olive or coconut oil
- 1 teaspoon sea salt
- 2 tablespoons psyllium husk powder

Preheat the oven to 360 degrees and prepare and measure all of the ingredients. Combine all ingredients, except for the water and psyllium husk, into a blender or food processor and blend until all are evenly ground. Add the water and psyllium husk powder and continue to mix. Prepare a small, rectangular baking dish by lining or coating with coconut or olive oil and pour the mixture evenly. Bake for 55-60 minutes. Keep an eye on the oven during the last ten minutes to ensure that it is baking thoroughly. Allow the bread to cool slightly before slicing to serve.

This recipe can be modified by increasing the amount of some nuts and seeds to replace others. For example, if you do not want to include sunflower seeds, substitute by doubling almonds or pumpkin seeds or another item. Enhance the particular flavor (nuts and seeds) by doubling the portion of some and reducing one or two of the other options.

Simple Vegan Keto Bread

This recipe is simple, although it includes a few additional ingredients compared to the first option, and it has fewer nuts and seeds (a few can be added as an option if desired). This recipe includes two different types of flour: coconut and almond. These work well together with their texture for many recipes, including crepes and cakes. Guar gum is also used in this recipe, along with psyllium husk, as a way to thicken the dough.

- 1 cup of almond flour
- 1/8 cup of coconut flour
- 1/8 cup of ground linseed

- 5-6 tablespoons of water
- ¼ cup psyllium husk powder
- 1 tablespoon guar gum
- 1 tablespoon baking powder
- 1 teaspoon sea salt
- Dash of spices (sage, oregano, rosemary, etc.)
- 1/8 cup coconut oil
- 1 tablespoon apple cider vinegar
- 1 cup of water (separate from the 5-6 tablespoons mentioned above)

Preheat the oven to 400 degrees. Combine all of the dry ingredients, with the exception of the linseed, and mix everything in a medium bowl. In a separate bowl, combine the linseed and water (5-6 tablespoons) and set aside. After 10 minutes, check the thickness of the linseed mixture to ensure that it has thickened, and add it to the remaining dry ingredients. Add 1 cup of water and the apple cider vinegar. Continue to mix all ingredients and knead into a dough. Form small buns or loaves on a prepared baking sheet, coated in olive or coconut oil, and bake for 50-60 minutes. Check the progress between 50-60 minutes, and bake the bread for an extra 10-15 minutes after 60, if needed. Serve warm or cool. These can be sliced and toasted.

Adding Vegan Keto Bread to Your Regular Meals

Vegan keto bread can easily fit into any meal of the day or as a light snack, toasted with nut butter, vegan butter, or cream cheese. A bread with a more seedy, hearty texture will work well with soups and salads, and lighter breads make an excellent choice for breakfast. Light to medium bread buns work well with vegan burgers, and a lighter, thinner crepe-like wrap can also be good with breakfast or wraps (included in the breakfast recipes). In general, vegan keto bread can take the place of their carb-heavy versions. If one or two recipes are too heavy or unappealing, there are many other variations and recipes to consider. It's an opportunity to become acquainted with the "anatomy" of what makes a good bread to your taste, and experimenting with as many options as possible will provide a lot of choices, more than with regular bread!

Tools and Equipment for a Vegan Keto Diet

There are many gadgets, innovative kitchen appliances, and state-of-the-art blenders and juicers that can create anything imaginable. Fortunately, for the vegan keto diet, these can be helpful, though not completely necessary. Simple, easy-to-use tools and a good blender or food processor can take care of many recipes. Here are some standard, basic items to have when creating recipes:

- **A blender and food processor**. A handheld blender (or small, cup-sized) is a good idea for making quick, single-serve smoothies or milkshakes. A food processor is ideal for crushing nuts and seeds and combining ingredients (both wet and dry) for all your recipes.
- **Whisk**. This is a simple, handheld tool useful for mixing ingredients by hand.
- **Skillet (one medium, one large)**. Having at least two cast-iron skillets are great for stir fry dishes and making breakfast crepes or tofu scramble. Cast iron skillets are heated on low to medium heat (never above medium) with coconut, olive, or avocado oil before frying or sautéing meals.
- **Spatulas, large ladle, and forks**. Spatulas are used in mixing, flipping, and turning over foods while cooking. A strong wooden or stainless-steel spoon is good for stirring.
- **Glass or durable (reusable and resealable) plastic containers** to store, freeze, and refrigerate prepared foods and ingredients
- **Glass jars** for spices, herbs, teas, and other dry ingredients in your pantry

- **One or two strong, durable graters (one fine and one for larger pieces)** is ideal for shredding vegetables for patties, hash browns, and salads. Two graters, one of each size, is recommended to accommodate most recipes.
- **Stainless steel cooking pots (one medium and one large)** for soups and stews and making curries and similar sauces
- **Measuring utensils**, such as cups, teaspoons, and tablespoons are helpful in ensuring that all ingredients are measured accurately.
- **A good quality set of knives and a sharpener** for slicing vegetables, fruits, and baked goods

There are many other items that can be added, though these utensils, tools, and equipment are a good foundation for most recipes.

Special & Unique Ingredients to Consider for the Diet

If you are adventurous when it comes to trying new foods, spices, and meals from other cultures and regions, here are some tips to keep in mind to avoid adding unwanted carbs, meat products, or both. If you shop in a store that specializes in various Asian foods, you'll notice a lot of noodles and rice and starch-rich products, which should be avoided. Fortunately, there are a lot of keto and vegan-friendly options that make it easy, such as soy products (tofu, soy milk, and miso), fermented foods (kimchi cabbage and radishes are popular), and lots of greens. If you are having difficulty finding vegan keto-friendly foods at your local grocery store, look for a large or medium-sized Asian grocery store, which can offer many more options.

Bakeries and coffee shops offer a lot of sugary and carb-heavy foods, which should be eliminated, though some specialty bakeries are popping up in some cities that specialize in ketogenic, vegan, and gluten-free goods. These are worth checking out to find out which ingredients are used in their foods. Shops that specialize in food products that cater to specific dietary needs are often very willing to provide as much information possible to assure their customers that their foods have good in quality. Quality ingredients are the most important and should be reviewed before making final decisions on purchasing from one of these stores. Reading reviews and feedback is another good idea.

Delicatessens, local farmers markets, and grocers with fresh street-side produce are the best options, as they usually provide fresh and local goods. Delicatessens tend to feature meat, cheese, and dairy, though some may offer vegan alternatives as well.

Chapter 6: Frequently Asked Questions and Answers About the Vegan Keto Diet

How Does the Vegan Keto Diet Maximize Weight Loss?

Going both vegan and keto gives you the best of both diets. A plant-based diet is lower in trans and saturated fats and higher in healthier fats, which is better for your overall health. A vegan diet is also higher in fiber since it is entirely based on vegetation, which keeps metabolism regular and weight manageable. The ketogenic diet, on the other hand, reduces the amount of carbohydrates while increasing healthy fats and maintaining protein. This not only keeps your body healthy and strong, but it also increases fat burning through ketosis (described in chapter 1). While sticking with the plant-based foods and adapting to ketogenic eating at the same time, all of the benefits from both diets are combined to provide all the benefits to maximize weight loss and keep your weigh at a consistent level once your goal is achieved.

Will I Meet All of My Daily Nutritional Requirements?

It is important that all your daily requirements for nutrients are met in order to avoid developing deficiencies. Some of the most common deficiencies are vitamin D and B12, especially on a vegan diet, as dairy and meat contain one or both (many milk products are fortified with vitamin D). Other minerals and vitamins that can be challenging to get from a vegan diet are iron, protein, calcium, and magnesium. Fortunately, a lot of soy products and non-dairy, vegan milks contain vitamin D and B12. Dark green vegetables are among the best sources for minerals, including iron, which is often low in vegan diets. Keeping track of the foods you eat and the nutritional value for each are important in maintaining a balanced diet.

Is it an Easy Diet to Follow?

There are challenges to following a vegan keto diet, though there are ways to make it easier to adapt and to follow. One thought to keep in mind when shopping is that every regular food item has a vegan keto alternative. For butter, there is a nut butter, vegan butter, or oil as an alternative. For sugar, there are low-carb sweeteners, and in place of dairy, there are coconut and soy-based options. The list and availability of both keto and vegan foods is continually growing and improving over time. It's beneficial to research as much as possible about natural supplements and vitamins while avoiding synthetic and processed versions, which can appear similar to their natural counterparts.

What Happens if I "Cheat" by Eating Animal-Based or High-Carb Food?

This will occur from time to time, either by accident or when there is a special meal or occasion where vegan keto food options are not readily available. Sometimes, it can be impossible to plan ahead for special dietary requests. This can occur when you are on vacation or in an unfamiliar region with a completely different assortment of fruits and vegetables. In these situations, it's best to stick with vegan first, as much as possible. And then, avoid carbs when they are obvious, and simply do not worry about reducing carbs until after the occasion. Remember that this is a temporary situation, not a setback or a failure. Everyone can take a break or "carb up" (increase carbohydrate intake) for a variety of reasons, such as vigorous exercise, hiking, cycling, marathons, etc. There is always another opportunity to jump back into vegan keto.

Chapter 7: Meal Planning and Preparation

The essential food items you need to start the diet and prepare for meal planning include a 4-week vegan keto masterplan.

Meal planning and preparation are the most important part of following and sticking to a healthy vegan keto diet. This plan is a guide to get you started on meal choices, with all of the corresponding recipes listed in the following chapter, under various meals of the day. To keep the plan easier to follow, just breakfast, lunch, and dinner are listed. Vegan keto snacks and desserts, while they are significantly good, should not be eaten in excess. The main focus is on the three main meals of the day.

First Week: Keeping it Simple

Week 1	Su	M	T	W	T	F	Sa
Breakfast	Avocado Coconut power smoothie	Tofu scramble	Curried Tofu scramble	Fruit and Coconut yogurt cup	Tofu scramble	Curried Tofu scramble	Vegan Keto breakfast bagels
Lunch	Avocado and tofu bake	Avocado Toast	Mediterranean sandwich	Avocado Toast	Sesame tofu bake	Peanut butter and toast	Eggplant with vegan cheese
Dinner	Butternut squash soup	Broccoli and cauliflower rice	Zucchini noodle pasta	Butternut squash baked with smoked tofu	Curried pumpkin soup	Vegan Keto platter	Vegan keto chili

Second Week: Adding More Options

Week 2	Su	M	T	W	T	F	S
Breakfast	Avocado Coconut power smoothie	Tofu scramble	Vegan keto breakfast bagels	Fruit and Coconut yogurt cup	Tofu scramble	Curried Tofu scramble	Vegan Keto breakfast bagels
Lunch	Avocado and tofu bake	Curried cabbage	Pizza stuffed peppers	Tandoori tempeh	Fried mushrooms and Brussel sprouts		
Dinner	Vegan keto chili (leftover from Sat)	Cauliflower macaroni and cheese					

Third Week: Getting Creative

Week 3	Su	M	T	W	T	F	S
Breakfast	Skillet breakfast	Chia pudding	Curried Tofu scramble	Fruit and Coconut yogurt cup	Skillet breakfast	Vegan keto crepes	Shakshuka
Lunch	Avocado and tofu bake	Zucchini noodles and avocado sauce	Curried tempeh and snow peas	Avocado toast	Pizza stuffed peppers	Smoked tofu and arugula	Peanut butter and toast
Dinner	Skillet meal (choice of 1-11)						

Fourth Week: Staying on Track

Week 4	Su	M	T	W	T	F	S
Breakfast	Chia pudding	Avocado smoothie	Tofu scramble	Fruit and coconut yogurt cup	Tofu scramble	Curried Tofu scramble	Tofu and spinach pies
Lunch	Peanut butter and toast	Curried cabbage	Sesame tofu bake	Grilled "cheese"	Lettuce sandwich wrap	Tandoori tempeh	Curried broccoli and kale soup
Dinner	Vegan moussaka	Skillet meal (choice of 1-11)					Cauliflower macaroni and cheese

Vegan Keto Recipes

Breakfast

Tofu Scramble

Tofu is a superfood that can take the place of many types of meat and dairy products, including eggs, which are frequently used in breakfast meals. The consistency of tofu can vary from soft to firm, depending on the dish you create. Tofu takes on any flavor and is best marinated overnight or for a few hours to absorb spices, juices, or broth to combine the tastes together before cooking. To prepare this dish, soak one block of firm tofu in a container or bowl of vegetable broth, black pepper, and salt. The ingredients are simple, easy to find, and can be modified to add spice or different flavors:

- 2 cups of vegetable broth
- One block of firm tofu, or the equivalent
- 2 teaspoons of turmeric
- 1 teaspoon salt
- 1 teaspoon black pepper

Wash and soak the block of tofu in a bowl of vegetable broth so that it is fully immersed. Add a dash of salt and pepper and mix into the broth before marinating. Keep in a closed container and leave in the refrigerator overnight so that it is ready for breakfast in the morning. Heat the skillet on medium and add turmeric and a couple of tablespoons of vegetable broth from the marinated tofu. Drain the tofu and reserve ½ cup of liquid. Mash the tofu and add another teaspoon of turmeric, salt, and black pepper and mix well, then transfer the mashed tofu to the skillet and cook. The combination of broth and turmeric will give the tofu a golden appearance, similar to scrambled eggs. The tofu takes roughly 5-7 minutes to cook fully and can be enjoyed right away.

There are some tasty ingredients to consider for enhancing the flavor:

- Chili pepper or flakes
- Chopped or sliced green peppers and onions: a small portion of these can be fried into the tofu scramble
- Spinach (fresh or frozen)
- Fried mushrooms (any variety)

Curried Tofu Scramble

This dish is a variation on the regular version, which marinates the tofu in curry spice the night before, along with all the ingredients in the recipe above. Just like the regular tofu scramble, this spicier option can include the same vegetables above and a few others for consideration:

- Okra
- Red peppers
- Green beans

Add the following spices to the vegetable broth and tofu to marinate overnight. Drain the next morning and retain ½ cup for frying the tofu.

- Two tablespoons of curry powder or paste
- 1 teaspoon garlic powder or salt
- 2-3 bay leaves, crushed
- 1 teaspoon chili powder or flakes
- Black pepper and salt (just a dash or more, depending on your preference)
- ½ teaspoon garam masala (optional)
- 1 teaspoon turmeric
- 1 teaspoon cumin

Prepare in a skillet like the regular tofu scramble and serve with fresh coriander or parsley.

Avocado Coconut Power Smoothie

Smoothies are easy, healthy, and delicious any time of day, and especially a good option for breakfast. They provide a good dose of daily nutrients in a fraction of time it takes to prepare a full meal. As this is the first meal of the day, it's important to include a lot of nutrients and healthy fats, which both coconut and avocado provide. Only a few key ingredients are required for this quick smoothie:

- 1 medium or large ripe avocado
- 1 can of coconut (or the equivalent – roughly 1 ½ cups)
- ¼ cup coconut cream (unsweetened)
- 2 tablespoons monk fruit, swerve or stevia
- 2 tablespoons of collagen protein powder (vanilla flavor)

Combine the fleshy parts of the avocados, coconut milk, cream in a blender and mix until all of the ingredients are smooth. If the blend is not thick enough, add more coconut cream or half of another avocado to thicken the smoothie. Add the sweetener and collagen powder, then continue to mix until evenly combined and serve. Garnish with unsweetened coconut flakes, if desired.

If you want to add more protein to this recipe, add a dollop of sesame, almond, or peanut butter (unsweetened, no additives). Hemp and flaxseeds or oil is another good option. MCT or coconut oil will add more healthy fats to this smoothie. For a good boost of protein, healthy fats, and nutrients, feel free to add all of the above.

Vegan Keto Crepes

Enjoying crepes does not have to be a thing of the past because there is a low-carb alternative that is just as tasty, with some delicious toppings as well. Crepes, like pancakes, are prepared with whole wheat flour, which is replaced with almond and coconut flour, which has an easy consistency to work with for many vegan and keto baking recipes. This crepe recipe specifically can also be used as roti or wrap for stir fry and curries as a flatbread. Eggs can be replaced with coconut cream and flaxseeds:

- 2 tablespoons coconut cream mixed with flaxseeds (mix separately, preferably in a blender to combine well)
- ¾ cup almond milk
- ½ cup water
- 1 cup almond flour
- 1-2 tablespoons of monk fruit, stevia or a similar low-carb sweetener
- Olive or coconut oil for frying (as much as needed)

Heat the skillet on medium and mix the sweetener and almond flour in a large or medium bowl, whichever you prefer. Add into the bowl the flaxseed mix, coconut cream, water, and almond milk and continue to stir. Ensure all ingredients are combined equally and that the mixture is not too thick but light and slightly thicker than milk. Once the oil is heated, pour the equivalent of

½ cup of the mixture and fry for 2 minutes or until the crepe can be lifted easily (without breaking apart) with a spatula. Gently flip the crepe and cook the opposite side. Once you achieve a golden hue on both sides, transfer to a plate, add the topping of your choice, and fold.

- Whipped coconut cream (store-bought coconut whipping cream or made with a sweetener and ½ cup of cream in an electric blender)
- Cinnamon
- Fresh or lightly stewed berries and rhubarb
- Nut butter spread (almond, peanut or hazelnut butter)
- Cocoa powder sprinkled on the crepe or melted dark chocolate (unsweetened). Combine melted cocoa or chocolate with nut butter for another option
- Sliced avocado drizzled in coconut cream and sesame seeds
- Low-carb syrup

Almond flour is the most versatile and easy to use low-carb flour for vegan keto baking, though it can be expensive. Another option to consider is combining a ½ cup of coconut flour with ½ cup almond flour. Coconut flour is drier and more challenging to work with on its own, though it can be a good combination with almond and is less costly. Purchasing both flours in bulk is another option to keep within a budget and have enough to prepare a variety of recipes.

Fruit and Coconut Yogurt Cup

This delicious and quick breakfast can be prepared with all plant-based and natural ingredients without all the carbohydrates. While many fruits contain a lot of carbs, berries tend to rank low on this scale, which makes them acceptable as a tasty addition to many meals, either fresh or frozen. In this recipe, fresh, locally harvested berries work best. The cup can be mixed or layered, beginning with the fruit, then the yogurt, followed by toppings:

- 1 cup of coconut-cultured yogurt (plain or vanilla)
- ½ cup keto granola (see recipe later)
- 1 cup of fresh berries (blueberries, strawberries, raspberries, blackberries, or a combination of these)

In a tall glass or cup, add the fruit to the bottom, followed by a second layer of yogurt. Add the keto granola as a topping, and add these options:

- Dark, unsweetened cocoa or chocolate chips or shavings
- Shredded coconut or flakes (unsweetened)
- Flax and hemp seeds
- Crushed peanuts or almonds
- Cinnamon

For an additional fruit option, rhubarb is a low-carb fruit that is very sour in taste and which can be stewed and sweetened with monk fruit or another low-carb sweetener. Rhubarb compliments the sweetness of the berries as well for a good mix either below the yogurt or mixed together and garnished with the toppings of your choice.

To add more protein to this serving, soak ¼ cup of chia seeds in the yogurt for at least two hours or overnight, then use the thickened mixture to top the berries, or mix them together. The chocolate or coconut flakes can similarly be added to the yogurt and blended instead of a topping.

Vegan Keto Breakfast Bagels

Bagels are carb-heavy, as well as other baked bread and pastries, and a ketogenic, plant-based option can be substituted to satisfy this craving. In keto baking, wheat flour is typically switched to coconut and almond flour. Eggs, cheese, and butter are also typically used to prepare keto bagels and other baked goods, which can be simply replaced with plant-based alternatives, without compromising flavor:

- 1/3 cup of ground flaxseeds
- ½ cup of sesame butter
- ¼ cup psyllium powder or collagen powder (or both combined into ¼ cup)
- 1 tablespoon of water
- 1 tablespoon of baking powder
- Sesame seeds

Combine all the dry ingredients (flaxseeds, collagen or psyllium powder, and baking powder) in a medium bowl and mix well. The oven must be warmed to 380 degrees as you prepare the ingredients. In a separate bowl, whisk the water and sesame butter thoroughly, then add to the dry ingredients. Continue to mix with a spoon or by hand until it becomes a dough and can be kneaded. Prepare a baking tray and line with parchment paper. Form bagel-shaped molds by hand or by rolling into a 3" ball, gently flattening on the paper and cutting out a 1" hole in the center. Continue until all the mixture is used, which should make about 4-6 small, thin bagels. Bake the bagels for 45 minutes or when they have become slightly crispy and golden brown. Slice, toast, or enjoy fresh out of the oven with one of the following toppings:

- Avocado and vegan cheese
- Nut butter spread (peanut or hazelnut butter)
- Tomato, basil leaves, and avocado slices

To add more flavor inside the bagels and for a sweeter option, combine 2 tablespoons of low-carb sweetener and 1 teaspoon of cinnamon powder for cinnamon bagels. For "everything" bagels, combine poppy seeds, sesame seeds, dried garlic, and onion powder in a small bowl and add as a topping to the bagel shapes just before baking.

Chia Pudding (Vanilla)

Chia seeds are considered a "superfood" due to the many health benefits they provide as a part of a regular diet or meal plan. One of the most popular ways to enjoy them is by adding the seeds to a pudding recipe. They provide a good source of fiber, protein, and calcium, and help improve digestion, cardiovascular health, and weight loss. This chia pudding is a basic, vanilla recipe, though many flavors can be added to change the taste and texture:

- ½ cup of chia seeds (any variety)
- 1 teaspoon vanilla
- 1 cup of coconut milk
- 1-2 teaspoons cinnamon (optional topping)
- ¼ cup stevia, monk fruit or similar low-carb sweetener
- 1 cup of coconut cream (similar to the thickness in dairy full fat cream)

Combine the coconut milk, cream, and sweetener and whisk together gently in a medium bowl, then add the vanilla and chia seeds and continue to mix. Blend carefully to ensure all the chia seeds are evenly spaced in the mixture. Some of the seeds may stick to the utensils and sides of the bowl. If this occurs, gently slide them back into the mixture and stir until all ingredients are even. Move the liquid to a sealable container and refrigerate overnight and enjoy in the morning with a sprinkle of cinnamon on top of each serving.

The toppings and flavors for chia pudding options are limitless, and they provide a fun and healthy way to enjoy this highly nutritious treat.

- Add melted dark, unsweetened chocolate (approximately ¼ cup) to the ingredients for a chocolate or cocoa pudding
- Fresh berries can be added to the mix or as a topping. If frozen berries are available, blend with the coconut milk and cream mixture, before adding the chia seeds, sweetener, and vanilla
- Cardamom spice can be used in place of cinnamon
- A blend of or one of these nuts can make a delicious addition to the pudding, as a topping or mixed with the chia seeds: almonds, macadamia nuts, hazelnuts, peanuts, or walnuts
- Blend the coconut cream and milk with pumpkin puree (about ½ cup), then add the remaining ingredients in the original recipe. This variation can be topped with roasted pumpkin seeds
- Hemp hearts and MCT oil make excellent supplements to chia pudding

The advantage of this recipe is having different options and how simple it is to make. Chia pudding can be a regular breakfast option, a snack, or a meal substitute in situations where you need a quick, nutritious solution.

Shakshuka

This dish is popular in Middle Eastern cuisine. Traditionally, this dish is comprised of eggs poached in a spicy tomato sauce combined with vegetables and meat, peppers, and herbs, sometimes topped with cheese. For the ketogenic diet, this meal works perfectly, and it can easily be adapted to fit the vegan keto diet with a few modifications to the ingredients:

- firm tofu, half a block (cubed, 1 or 2-inches)
- 1 small can of tomatoes
- 1 bell pepper, diced
- ½ cup diced tomatoes (optional)
- 1 garlic clove, crushed
- 1 tablespoon chili pepper powder or flakes
- 1 tablespoon cumin seeds
- Dash of black pepper and salt (sea salt or pink Himalayan salt)
- Parsley for garnish
- 2-3 tablespoons of olive oil

Heat a skillet on low to medium heat and add 2-3 tablespoons of olive oil and all of the spices, herbs and cumin seeds. Fry for 2-3 minutes, then add garlic and bell pepper and continue to fry for 2-3 more minutes. Decrease the heat to low, and add the diced tomatoes and tomato sauce. Stir the ingredients into the sauce and let it stew for 10 minutes while preparing the tofu.

Note: Tofu can be marinated in tomato sauce or vegetable broth the night before to add flavor or simply use as is.

In a separate, small skillet, add one tablespoon of olive oil and coat the pan evenly. Heat on medium heat and add tofu cubes and increase heat to sear. Remove the skillet from the heat once the tofu is fully cooked and add the seared tofu to the spiced tomato sauce, carefully stirring in the pieces and coating them evenly with sauce.

Skillet Breakfast

Stir fry meals and skillet dishes are not just for lunch or dinner. Fresh peppers, mushrooms, and other vegetables can combine well in a skillet for an easy, healthy first meal of the day in a matter of minutes. If you enjoy a quick meal before you leave for work, cut the vegetables the night before and store in a container; airtight would be best. Leave it overnight in the fridge.

- 2 tablespoons sesame seeds
- 4-5 small or medium mushrooms, sliced
- 2-3 basil leaves
- 1 green pepper sliced lengthwise into strips
- 2 tablespoons of olive oil
- Smoked tofu or tempeh (half a block or package)
- 2 stalks of celery, diced into small 1" pieces

Heat the skillet and add olive oil for approximately one minute on a medium level. Add celery first, followed by tofu or tempeh, then green peppers, and basil leaves. Leave mushrooms to add once most of the vegetables and tofu are nearly cooked yet crunchy, and continue to sauté it on low to medium heat. Sprinkle sesame seeds on top and gently mix into the ingredients before serving.

If you like a spicy version of this dish, add chili peppers or flakes or one sliced jalapeno pepper. For a curried flavor, add ½ cup of coconut milk and 2 tablespoons of curry powder in between adding the remaining ingredients and the celery.

Turnip Hash Browns

Potatoes are often a staple in breakfast meals as hash browns or home fries. They are also high in carbs and starch. Turnips or rutabaga can be a good alternative: not only are they low in carbs, but they are also high in fiber and nutrients and flavor. They can be shredded similarly to potatoes to make hash browns in a skillet or baked in the oven. Spices, herbs, and salt can enhance the taste. Eggs are usually used to bind the shredded vegetable together, along with flour, though these ingredients can be easily switched to a lower-carb option:

- 1 medium rutabaga or turnip
- 2 tablespoons of water
- 1 tablespoon almond flour
- Dash of salt
- Black pepper

With a large shredder, grate the turnip or rutabaga into large shredded pieces. A smaller, finer grater can be used, though a large one will create a better texture for frying on the skillet. In a medium bowl, combine the grated turnip with water, flour, salt, and pepper and mix thoroughly until it is moist and slightly sticky. On medium-low heat, warm a skillet and pour some olive oil. Scoop two tablespoons of the mix onto the hasted skillet. Flatten gently with the back of the spoon and fry for 2 minutes.

Using a spatula, carefully flip the patty over and continue to fry for another 2 or 3 minutes.

What if the patty falls apart? Not a problem! Simply chop up the turnip mix and continue to try evenly, turning the mixture over until golden and slightly crispy. Serve as a side with smoked tofu and tofu scramble or on its own with a generous dollop of coconut yogurt.

There are other options to enhance the flavor:

- Add 1-2 tablespoons of very fine diced onion or garlic
- Fresh or dried herbs: dill, rosemary or paprika
- Spice it up with chili or cayenne pepper

Mix the desired option(s) into the batter before frying. Dried herbs can also be sprinkled on top as a garnish.

Protein Peanut Butter and Chocolate Breakfast Bites

These are quick and easy on-the-go breakfast bites that can be made within a few minutes or the night before. It's best to prepare at least two hours in advance to ensure they can chill in the refrigerator. This recipe includes peanut butter, which can be substituted for hazelnut or almond butter (they both have similar consistencies and work just as well). The ingredients are simple and easy to find in bulk or the dried goods area of the grocery store:

- 1 teaspoon MCT or coconut oil
- 2 cups of peanut butter
- ½ cup coconut flour
- ¼ cup low-carb sweetener (monk fruit or stevia)
- 1 cup melted dark chocolate (unsweetened) or cocoa

Prepare a medium or large baking tray (or similar-sized tray) by placing a baking or parchment paper. Place MCT or coconut oil, peanut butter, coconut flour, and sweetener in a medium bowl and combine. Mix thoroughly until all of the ingredients are evenly combined. Form small ball shapes and refrigerate for approximately one hour or freeze for 15 minutes. While the energy balls chill, prepare the chocolate by melting the equivalent of 1 cup dark, unsweetened (keto-friendly) chocolate or cocoa on low heat. Add a teaspoon of coconut oil and mix with a fork as the chocolate melts. If you have a powdered cocoa powder instead, this can be prepared by mixing with melted coconut oil (one or two teaspoons) in a small bowl. Add more chocolate or cocoa until there is enough to coat each one of the balls. When they are ready, remove them from the refrigerator or freezer and evenly coat each of them with chocolate and set aside. Once they are all coated, chill for at least half an hour, and they will be ready to enjoy.

If you want to get creative with these bites, they can be sprinkled with crushed peanuts, almonds, pistachios, or coconut flakes. Adding a dash of sea salt is another great option, for a "salted" taste.

Tofu and Spinach Breakfast Pies

These are prepared using an oven and a muffin tray with cup liners. Just like the egg and spinach bites or small pies, this recipe substitutes with tofu and spinach. These can be made the night before, refrigerated, and easily reheated in the morning. If made in the morning, give yourself some extra time to prepare and gauge how much time you need, especially if you have a busy schedule.

Just as with tofu scramble, this recipe works best when the tofu is marinated the night before. Although this is optional, it will create a stronger taste and provides a good way to infuse different spices with the tofu to soak overnight, as well as in the preparation the next morning. The ingredients are as follows:

- 1 block of tofu
- 1 teaspoon black pepper
- ¼ cup of vegetable broth
- ½ cup frozen (thawed) or fresh spinach (chopped)
- 2 tablespoons turmeric (add more to marinate with vegetable broth the night before, as well as when preparing the pies)
- 1 teaspoon diced onion
- 1 teaspoon sea salt
- Optional spices: thyme, dill, paprika, chili pepper

The oven must be ready at 350 degrees before baking. Prepare a muffin tray by placing cup liners (either disposable or reusable). In a medium bowl, add the block of tofu and mash with a fork. If marinated the night before, drain and keep ¼ cup of the fluid (broth with your choice of spices) or simply add the same amount of broth at that time and mix together. Continue to mash the tofu until it resembles a scrambled-like texture. Add the spinach, black pepper, salt, turmeric, and onion. It desired, add another 1 or 2 tablespoons of broth. Mix together thoroughly and transfer into a blender. Mix until as smooth as possible, then scoop to fill each muffin liner halfway. The recipe should yield approximately six pies. Bake for approximately 12-14 minutes, or until the texture resembles a mini quiche. If needed, bake for another 5-6 minutes. Garnish the top with dill or parsley and serve warm, or chill it and serve within the next 2 days.

Fruit and Keto Granola With Coconut Milk

This is an easy dish to prepare by simply combining the ingredients and enjoying with cold coconut (or almond) milk in the morning. The granola recipe under "snacks" can be added to this dish, or the following items can be dry roasted, cooled, and added to the milk.

- ¼ cup almond slivers
- ½ cup coconut flakes (unsweetened)

Roast the almonds and coconut in a skillet on medium for approximately 2-3 minutes until the ingredients brown, then remove it from the stove and add in a tablespoon of chia seeds and any other seeds or nuts you desire. Or you can simply add 1 cup of the vegan keto granola recipe to 1 cup of fresh fruit, and pour some coconut milk to cover most of the mix to enjoy. Dark chocolate or cocoa chips can be added as a topping.

Crispy Flaxseed Waffles

If you have a waffle iron, it doesn't have to be ignored once you switch to a vegan keto diet. This recipe is a new way to put this appliance to work, while providing a nourishing meal:

- 1 teaspoon baking powder
- 2 cups ground flaxseeds
- ½ cup water (separate)
- ½ cup avocado oil, olive oil, or coconut oil
- 1 teaspoon sea salt
- ¼ cup warm water combined with 3 tablespoons ground flaxseeds
- 1 teaspoon cinnamon or cardamom spice

Combine and mix the flaxseeds, baking powder, salt, and cinnamon or cardamom spice thoroughly in a medium bowl. Blend the wet ingredients (water, oil, and flaxseed-water mixture) in a food processor or blender until frothy, then add to the bowl of dry ingredients (already mixed). As these two batches of mixed ingredients are stirred together, they will thicken (this is exactly what you want to happen!). Heat the waffle iron and pour the batter to coat the inside, then close the lid and cook. Once the waffle is done, serve with coconut cream, low-carb syrup, or cinnamon powder. Fresh berries are another excellent option.

Vegan Keto Porridge

If you crave the comfort of a warm bowl of porridge or hot cereal, especially on a cold morning, this grain-free, low-carb recipe will provide that fix. As with many keto recipes, hemp hearts and flaxseeds are used to replace oats and other high-carb grains. Non-dairy milk is also added:

- ½ cup hemp hearts
- 1 cup of almond or coconut milk
- 2 tablespoons chia seeds
- 1 tablespoon monk fruit
- ¼ teaspoon vanilla extract
- ¼ teaspoon of cinnamon
- Dash of salt
- 3 tablespoons ground flaxseeds

Combine all the ingredients, including the non-dairy milk and refrigerate overnight in a sealed container. On the next morning, pour the ingredients into a small or medium cooking pot and heat on low to medium heat, stirring all of the ingredients until the cereal is brought to boil. Once it is ready, remove from heat and serve topped with slivered almonds or coconut flakes.

Pumpkin Pancakes

These are simple and easy to prepare for a unique spin on regular breakfast or weekend brunch. This recipe requires low-carb flour and canned or fresh pumpkin puree:

- ½ cup of pumpkin puree (canned or fresh)
- 1 teaspoon cinnamon
- 1 teaspoon nutmeg
- 1 teaspoon monk fruit (optional)
- 1 cup coconut milk
- 1 cup almond flour
- ½ cup coconut flour
- 2 tablespoons coconut or olive oil

Pour some olive or coconut oil in a warmed medium-sized skillet, and keep it on medium heat while you prepare a large bowl where you combine and mix all the ingredients. Use an electric or handheld whisk for best results. Blend well and avoid leaving any lumps or clusters of dried ingredients. Add a few teaspoons of water if the batter seems too runny for you. If it's too thick like a paste, add one or two tablespoons of almond flour. The batter should be thin enough to pour onto the skillet to make a 3-4-inch diameter pancake. Fry the batter for 1-2 minutes on each side. Serve with a sprinkle of cinnamon, nutmeg, fresh fruit, low-carb syrup, and coconut cream.

Cocoa Crepes Cocoa Crepes

If you enjoy dessert for breakfast, this is one option to consider. These crepes simply add cocoa powder to a simple three-ingredient vegan keto recipe as follows:

- 1 cup coconut milk
- ¼ cup cocoa powder
- 1 cup almond flour
- 2 tablespoons coconut or olive oil
- 1 cup coconut flour

Warm the skillet on medium-high heat, and pour the oil of your choice. While heating the pan, prepare all ingredients, and place them into a large bowl. Using a wire whisk or handheld mixer, and mix thoroughly all the ingredients to create a batter that is thinner or more runny than the pancake. Pour the batter into the skillet and cook for 1-2 minutes on each side. Serve with coconut cream or sprinkle with cocoa.

Pumpkin Protein Breakfast Smoothie

Bananas are often added to smoothies for their thickening effect. Pumpkin puree can provide a low-carb replacement for bananas in recipes. In this smoothie, pumpkin and almond butter provide a strong boost of fiber and protein to start off the day:

- 1 cup coconut or almond milk
- 2 tablespoons almond butter
- ½ cup pumpkin puree
- 2 tablespoons low-carb sweetener

Combine all ingredients in a blender and mix well for 30 seconds to one minute. Serve for breakfast or before a workout.

Almond and Pistachio Power Bars

These are energy bars that are made raw the night before and chilled for best results. The ingredients are simply blended in a food processor.

- 1 cup almond butter
- 2 teaspoons low-carb sweetener (monk fruit or stevia)
- ½ cup ground pistachios
- 2 tablespoons almond flour
- Dash of sea salt
- ½ teaspoon MCT oil

Prepare all ingredients and then combine and mix in a large or medium bowl. Make sure all the ground nuts and dry items are blended well into the almond butter using a fork. Prepare a small, square baking pan by adding the mixture and evening spreading to all sides and corners. Refrigerate for at least two hours, then remove and slice into bars. These are best made at night and refrigerated until the morning.

Other variations on this recipe include added shredded coconut or substituting pistachios for crushed walnuts or pecans. Almond butter can easily be switched to peanut, hazelnut, or sesame butter.

Tofu Berry Smoothie

Many recipes involving tofu require the firm or extra firm variety. Soft tofu is also an option for soups, sauces, and puddings. It can usually be found alongside many other tofu and meat-free options in the produce aisle. If you plan to use soft tofu, avoid choosing flavored puddings or desserts, as they are high in sugar. This smoothie adds a plain, unsweetened soft tofu to blend with berries. Since tofu is already high in protein and calcium, there is no need to add any supplements:

- 1 cup tofu
- 1 cup berries (fresh or frozen, any variety or mix)
- 1 teaspoon low-carb sweetener
- ½ cup almond milk

Combine ingredients in a blender and mix well for 30 seconds to one minute before serving.

Snacks

When going on a diet, including vegan ketogenic, it doesn't have to mean skipping snacks. Snacking in between meals or when you need an extra jolt of energy can be a great way to add more nutrients to your daily intake. There are plenty of tasty options, as well.

Kale chips

Baked kale chips are a delicious and healthy snack that's very easy to prepare. Kale is naturally bitter to taste, but that is nothing compared to its goodness. It contains plenty of vitamins, in addition to iron and calcium. One bunch of kale (any variety: black, green, or purple) can be used for chips. Any texture, from flat to extra curly is acceptable, as long as each piece is evenly coated in olive oil. The recipe only requires three main ingredients:

- One bunch of kale (any variety)
- Salt (sea salt or pink Himalayan salt is preferred)
- Olive oil (avocado or coconut oil is also acceptable)

Remove the stems from a bunch of kale and slice the leaves into small, 1 to 2- inch bite-sized pieces. If you need to wash the kale, make sure it is thoroughly dried before proceeding to the next step. While preparing the kale leaves, warm the oven to 350 degrees. Coat each piece of kale evenly and lightly in olive oil.

Prepare a baking tray and line with parchment paper. Evenly space the coated kale pieces, then sprinkle salt over all of them. Bake for 10 minutes when the oven is ready. Depending on the oven and size of kale, the cooking time can vary from 8-11 minutes. Monitor the chips carefully, as they can burn easily, within an extra minute or so. A couple of small batches may be a good idea as a "trial run" to determine the exact timing for each batch. Once this is established, making kale chips is one of the easiest recipes, and the results are addictive!

There are variations on this recipe, while keeping them both vegan and ketogenic:

- Add cumin and garam masala as a dried spice, along with salt, prior to baking.
- Chili pepper is a great way to spice up these chips, either in place of salt or mixed with it.
- Vegan parmesan or other dried cheese can be used to coat the kale to create a more "cheese" chip-like flavor. This may take a minute or two longer to bake.
- Garlic powder or salt, onion powder, paprika, and other similar spices can be used in combination or on their own to customize the flavor.

The best thing about kale chips? They don't take long to bake and do not require a dehydrator, though this can be used if desired. Kale chips take a fraction of time from preparation to finish than other vegetables, such as zucchini and other vegetables. This is because of the low content of water or moisture in kale.

Guacamole

This avocado-based dip can be used as a side for breakfast, as a dip with homemade vegetable chips or simply enjoyed on its own. It's completely plant-based and versatile for any meal of the day. The best avocadoes to use are very ripe and soft so that the fleshy part of the fruit can be mashed and mixed well with the other ingredients. There are only a few items needed to make a tasty guacamole:

- 2 medium or large sized avocadoes
- 2 tablespoons of olive oil (MCT or coconut oil can be used instead, or one tablespoon of each)
- Black pepper and salt
- 2 tablespoons lemon juice (or lime, if you prefer)
- Cilantro or parsley

Slice both avocadoes and remove their pits and scoop out the fleshy inside to a small bowl. Mash the avocado flesh well so that it is as smooth as possible, then add the oil, lime, or lemon juice, pepper, and salt, and continue to mix it thoroughly so that all ingredients are combined evenly. Cilantro and parsley can be chopped finely and added to the mix and topped as a garnish.

Vegan Keto Granola

Granola is typically made with oats, which are very high in carbohydrates. There is a low-carb option, which includes mixing a combination of nuts, seeds, and dried coconut flakes. There are some variations to this mix, which can be enjoyed as a cold cereal, with milk or coconut cultured yogurt, or as a topping on a dessert. The ingredients are easy to find, and can usually be found in bulk stores and regular supermarkets:

- 1 cup pumpkin seeds (toasted or plain)
- 1 teaspoon baking powder
- Dash of salt
- ½ cup hemp hearts
- ½ flaxseeds (whole or crushed)
- ¼ cup chia seeds (any variety)
- 1-2 tablespoons cinnamon
- 1-2 tablespoons psyllium husk and collagen powder
- ½ cup sunflower seeds
- Dried coconut flakes or shredded coconut (unsweetened)
- 1 cup of water

Before preparing the ingredients, start the oven and heat to 325 degrees. Prepare a baking sheet by lining it with parchment or baking paper. Place and grind all the seeds using a food processor or similar equipment. When the seeds are in smaller pieces (not powdered), mix in the remaining dry ingredients (everything but the water). Mix all of the ingredients evenly, then add the water and coat everything. Let sit for a few minutes to allow the granola to absorb the moisture. Spread the granola mixture evenly and thinly over the parchment paper and bake for 45 minutes. Monitor around 40-45 minutes, then remove from heat and break apart the granola with a spoon or spatula and bake for another half an hour (30 minutes). The mixture should be fully dry and crispy and ready to use once it is cooled. Remove from the oven and break up further, then store in a resealable container or use once it has cooled.

Keto granola is a tasty as a snack or a quick breakfast. It can be transferred to a reusable container as a snack on the run or enjoyed at home. This snack provides a lot of fiber and protein, which is ideal for a vigorous workout. For a more transferable snack option, other ingredients can be added to make it more of a "trail mix":

- Peanuts (raw or roasted)
- Almonds (slivered or crushed along with the cereal ingredients)
- Cocoa powder (sprinkled over the granola mix before baking – or used in place of cinnamon)

- Dried berries (unsweetened). Berries are typically low in carbs and can be added fresh or sun-dried in small amounts for a flavor boost
- Cardamom powder (instead of cinnamon)
- Sesame seeds

Chocolate Sesame Breakfast Smoothie

If you need a powerful boost in the morning, this is a simple and nutritious way to get it! Sesame butter is used in this smoothie instead of more common nut butters, such as peanut or almond butter. Sesame butter, or tahini, is commonly used in hummus and contains a lot of protein. Dark, unsweetened chocolate or raw cocoa can be used along with almond or coconut milk (or a combination of both):

- 2 cups almond or coconut milk (or one cup of each)
- 2 tablespoons of tahini or sesame butter
- ¼ cup dark chocolate unsweetened or raw cocoa (powder or melted in one teaspoon of coconut oil on low heat)
- 2 teaspoons monk fruit, stevia, or low-carb sweetener
- 2 teaspoons MCT or coconut oil
- 2-3 ice cubes

Place all the ingredients in a blender, placing the ice cubes last. Blend it for half a minute or so, until it runs smooth according to your favored consistency. Test the taste to decide if more sweetener is desired. This smoothie is also a good source of energy before a workout.

Coconut Bacon

If you crave bacon and miss the crispy flavor it provides, this recipe is an excellent alternative to substitute the real thing. This recipe involves smoking the coconut to create the distinctive flavor:

- 2 tablespoons of liquid smoke
- 1 tablespoon of soy sauce (unsweetened, no additives)
- 1 tablespoon liquid maple flavor
- 1 tablespoon water
- 3 cups of coconut flakes (unsweetened)

Before anything else, set the oven to 350 degrees temperature. In a medium bowl, combine liquid smoke, soy sauce, maple flavor, and water and mix. Add the coconut flakes and coat them evenly in the sauce, using a spoon to turn all the flakes to make sure they are all covered. Place a parchment paper on a medium or large baking sheet; spread the coated coconut flakes evenly on the sheet. Bake for 25 minutes and flip the flakes once every 5-7 minutes to ensure they all cook evenly. Remove from the oven once cooked, and allow it to cool before enjoying as a snack. They can be stored in a vaccum container or similar for up to 3-4 weeks or in the refrigerator.

Coconut Berry Smoothie

This is an easy way to get a boost of flavor and energy. This is prepared using coconut milk, fresh or frozen berries, and a low-carb sweetener:

- 2 cups unsweetened coconut milk
- 1 cup fresh or frozen berries (any variety or combination of strawberries, raspberries, blackberries, and blueberries)
- 1 tablespoon or sesame butter (for added protein)
- 2 tablespoons low-carb sweetener (stevia or monk fruit)

Blend all the ingredients for approximately 30 seconds to one minute. Remove once thoroughly blended to test the taste. Add more sweetener or other ingredients as desired. This smoothie is a great snack that can go into a portable cup for a road trip or commute to work.

Roasted Pumpkin Seeds

If you are planning on watching a movie or needs a light snack, this is a perfect way to replace chips or other high-carb options. During the autumn season when pumpkin is readily available, use the leftover seeds instead of discarding them:

- 2 cups of raw, dried pumpkin seeds
- 2 tablespoons olive oil
- Himalayan sea salt (enough to coat the seeds)

To get started, set the oven's temperature to 350 degrees and warm it up while you prepare the ingredients. In a large bowl, add the pumpkin seeds and olive oil, mixing well to ensure all seeds are coated. Add more oil if needed. Spread all the seeds on the baking sheet lined with baking paper and add some salt as desired. Place in the oven to bake for 10-12 minutes (more or less, until they are brown but not burnt). Roasted pumpkin seeds can be served after they have cooled a few minutes or stored and enjoyed up to 1 month.

Cinnamon Pumpkin Seeds

These are a variation on the regular roasted seeds, with sweetener and cinnamon instead of salt:

- 2 cups of raw, dried pumpkin seeds
- 2 tablespoons olive or coconut oil
- Cinnamon and low-carb sweetener (monk fruit is best) – just enough to coat the seeds

Follow the same recipe instructions for the regular roasted pumpkin seeds, coating first with low-carb sweetener, followed by cinnamon, or mixing both the cinnamon and sweetener in a bowl and coating the seeds with the blend. Bake at the same temperature and time frame until ready.

Rosemary Crisps

These are better than regular potato chips and with more flavor. Rosemary offers a unique taste to these crackers that pair well with vegan cheese, avocado, sliced tomatoes, and other toppings.

- 1 ½ cups almond flour
- ½ cup coconut flour
- ½ cup chopped pecan nuts
- 2 teaspoons baking soda
- 1 tablespoon fresh or dried rosemary
- ¼ cup ground flaxseeds
- 1 ¾ cups coconut milk (unsweetened)
- 3-4 tablespoons low-carb sweetener
- ¼ cup sesame seeds
- 1 teaspoon salt

Warm up the oven to 350 degrees. In a large or medium bowl, place both flours, salt, and baking soda and mix until well-incorporated. Add the sweetener and coconut milk and continue to stir. Then, add the remaining ingredients and continue to blend. Prepare one large baking sheet or two sheets by coating them in olive oil. Pour the batter the size a potato chip on the sheet and place in the oven. cook for approximately 30 minutes or until the crisp is in a golden brown hue. Remove from the oven and cool before serving. It is much easier to bake them thinner. If not consumed right away, it can be kept in an airtight bag in a pantry. They can be toasted or reheated in the oven if desired.

Lunches

Vegan keto lunches can be an easy meal to prepare for work, school, or at home. If you plan on eating at a cafeteria or nearby restaurant, keep in mind your options for keto and low-carb meals that are compatible with both a low-carb and plant-based diet. More restaurants and eateries, more than ever, are embracing new and modified menu items in response to a growing demand for both vegan and ketogenic meals and diets. The following food options can be found on many lunch menus:

- Vegetarian burgers, either soy or vegetable-based. If possible, note the brand and ingredients, as some plant-based burgers contain high-carb ingredients.

- Salads are a good option. Avoid sugary dressings and opt for balsamic vinegar or lime or lemon mixed with olive oil instead. Add nuts and seeds, and skip the cheese and dried fruit. Fresh berries are good.

- Side dishes may offer simple, healthy, low-carb, and vegetable options that can be combined (two or three) to make a complete meal. Examples of these are stewed spinach, pan-seared asparagus, fried zucchini, and baked squash. If you skip the main meal section of the menu and skim the sides, you'll be pleasantly surprised by some of the options available.

Preparing lunch in advance will not only help your budget; it will also keep you on track with the right food choices. There are many opportunities for lunch that are easy and light yet filling and satisfying.

Avocado and Tomato Salad

This is an easy and nutritious salad to prepare. The key to keeping the avocado from turning brown is by adding lime and olive oil. This can be prepared the night before, though it will be fresher if prepared earlier in the morning on the same day it is enjoyed. Choose the ingredients as fresh as possible. If the avocadoes are not ripe, they can still be sliced and added to the salad. These ingredients are easy to find and are best when they are in season or locally harvested whenever possible.

- 1 ½ cups of cherry tomatoes, sliced in half (as fresh as possible)
- 1 bunch arugula diced into small pieces
- 2 large avocadoes (if they are more firm than ripe, they can still be used, depending on your preference)
- 4-5 basil leaves, sliced (preferably fresh, or dried)
- 1-2 red, orange or yellow peppers sliced lengthwise

Combine and evenly mix the ingredients into a medium or large mixing bowl. In a small bowl, prepare the dressing by mixing the following ingredients:

- 1 tablespoon olive oil
- ½ teaspoon pink Himalayan salt
- 2 tablespoons balsamic vinegar
- 1-2 tablespoons lime or lemon juice

- ½ teaspoon black pepper
- 1 teaspoon of low-carb sweetener (preferably monk fruit)

Mix all of the ingredients and test the taste to ensure it is flavored to your desired level of sweetness or flavor combination. To serve the salad immediately, pour dressing over the salad and enjoy. If taking to lunch or consuming later in the day, add some lime or lemon juice to the salad to preserve the avocado, package the dressing in a small container separately, and mix just before eating.

There are some options to change the up the flavors to this dish. One option is to add roasted eggplant as a topping. To prepare the salad, slice a small eggplant into small disk shapes and rinse, then coat the slices in pink Himalayan salt, and set it aside for 20 minutes. Heat a skillet on low to medium heat. Rinse the eggplant slices in a colander once they have soaked in the salt for at least 20 minutes, which softens and prepares them for cooking. Fry on medium heat for approximately 5-6 minutes each side or until brown, then remove and add to the top of the salad. Zucchini can be similarly prepared in this way as an alternative topping, without coating in salt; simply slice the vegetable and fry it until golden.

Curried Tempeh and Snow Peas

Tempeh is fermented soy with a lot of nutrients and strong texture, making it a great feature of many dishes. In this recipe, the tempeh is marinated in curry spices overnight or for at least two hours before preparation. Snow peas can be either fresh or frozen. Other vegetables that work well in this dish include green peppers, asparagus, and zucchini, though these are optional (any low-carb vegetables can be added as desired):

- 2 cups of coconut milk
- 1/8 cup of curry powder
- 1 cup snow peas
- 1 tablespoon chili powder
- 1 block of tempeh (plain, unflavored)
- 1 tablespoon garlic salt
- ½ teaspoon black pepper
- 1-2 tablespoons of coconut or olive oil

Remove one block of tempeh from the package and slice into cubes. Combine the coconut milk, curry powder, and spices and mix well in a small bowl. Add the tempeh cubes to the bowl and make sure they are covered and coated evenly. Move all mixed ingredients to an airtight container and refrigerate overnight or at least for two hours to ensure they marinate the tempeh thoroughly.

When the tempeh is ready, heat on medium heat a pan or skillet with the oil of your choice. Drain the tempeh and retain the coconut milk and spice. Blend all of these in a small bowl. Fry the tempeh in the skillet, adding half of the coconut curry blend. Cook for approximately 10-12 minutes or until the tempeh is golden and slightly crispy. Add more of the coconut curry (or the remainder), and fry it for 2 minutes more before adding the snow peas. Fry the snow peas a bit; they still have to be crunchy when you serve them. Serve with salad or as a light meal on its own.

To enhance the flavor, garnish with crushed peanuts or sesame seeds. Fresh, chopped chives can also be added.

Avocado Toast

This can be an excellent breakfast, lunch, or brunch idea during a relaxing weekend. It involves using a keto bread of your choice (recipes in chapter 2) with vegan butter and fresh, ripe (not overripe) avocado.

- 2 slices of vegan keto bread
- 1 fresh, slightly ripe avocado, with both pit and skin removed and flesh cut into slices
- Vegan butter or olive oil (1 tablespoon)

Toast two slices of bread, and measure one tablespoon of olive oil in a small bowl or cup. Alternatively, vegan butter can be used instead of oil in the same amount. Coat both pieces of toast with butter (or oil), then cover in slices of avocado. Sprinkle with salt and pepper, then serve open-faced. If you want to add more to the overall flavor of the sandwich, top with fresh or dried basil leaves or sliced tomatoes.

Zucchini Noodles With Avocado Sauce

This dish combines spiral zucchini noodles or "zoodles" with a creamy avocado sauce, similar to Alfredo sauce. No cooking is required, and preparation is easy and fast, making this an ideal dish for lunch at work or over the weekend.

- 1 medium zucchini (spiraled into noodles)
- 1 cup dried basil
- ½ cup water
- 2 tablespoons of lemon juice
- 1 avocado (ripe)
- 8-10 sliced cherry tomatoes

In a blender or food processor, add the avocado, dried basil, water, and lemon juice and mix until smooth. Pour over the zucchini noodles on a plate and add in sliced cherry tomatoes. Sprinkle with basil and add dill if desired.

Fried Mushrooms and Brussel Sprouts

This dish combines a healthy portion of Brussel sprouts with mushrooms for a quick and easy skillet dish. If these vegetables are not your favorite, they can be substituted with asparagus or green beans for similar results. This meal is best served immediately after it is cooked:

- 1 cup of small mushrooms
- 2 tablespoons olive oil
- 1 teaspoon maple flavor
- 1 teaspoon sea salt
- 2 cups Brussel sprouts
- 1 tablespoon paprika
- 1 tablespoon vegan butter or coconut oil

Start the skillet on medium heat with some olive oil. Once warm and ready, cook the mushrooms for about 5 minutes, adding in the maple flavor, paprika, and sea salt. Continue cooking for another 5-10 minutes until the mushrooms are completely cooked and evenly coated in spices. Remove from heat and prepare a second skillet with vegan butter or coconut oil and preheat. Add the Brussel sprouts and water and cook until they are tender. That would be about 6-7 minutes. Drain, add the fried mushrooms, and combine. Serve warm.

Eggplant With Vegan "Cheese"

This is a simple version of eggplant parmesan, using vegan cheese as the substitute. To prepare the eggplant, slice into disk-like shapes, rinse in a colander, and coat evenly (both sides) with sea salt. Set aside for 20 minutes; the salt will soften the eggplant and prepare for the recipe. After 20 minutes, rinse in cold water and add to the recipe the following:

- 1 large eggplant, sliced into circles or disks
- Salt
- ½ almond flour
- ½ cup grated vegan cheese
- ¼ cup olive oil

Remove the prepared eggplant slices from the colander and coat lightly in olive oil. Mix and combine the almond flour and grated vegan cheese to coat the eggplant slices in a small bowl. Heat a skillet on medium and fry each slice on each side for about 5 minutes but not more than that. Byt then, they would be browned and ready to serve. Alternatively, the eggplant can be cooked in the oven at 350 degrees for 20-25 minutes or longer, depending on the size and thickness of the slices. Serve with soup, salad, or on its own as a light lunch.

Mediterranean Sandwich

This recipe works best with a light-textured vegan keto bread that can be easily toasted. For the Mediterranean flavor, a combination of olive paste, oil, and vegan cheese are used:

- Two slices of vegan keto bread
- 2-3 tablespoons of vegan cream cheese
- 1-2 tablespoons olive paste or pate
- 1-2 teaspoons olive oil
- Fresh basil leaves (as many as desired)
- ½ cup sliced cherry tomatoes

Toast both slices of bread and prepare the ingredients by mixing the olive paste and vegan cream cheese in a small bowl together. The olive oil can also be added to the bowl or simply used as "butter" for both slice of bread, whichever method is preferred. Spread the olive and vegan cheese blend on each slice of bread and top with fresh basil leaves and sliced cherry tomatoes

Tandoori Tempeh

This is a twist on the classic tandoori chicken dish, by simply replacing the meat with tempeh. For best results, marinate the tempeh overnight as follows:

- Slice tempeh into cubes, and add them to a bowl and coat in 2-3 tablespoons of tandoori paste

The following ingredients are used to make this dish:

- 1 ½ cups of coconut yogurt
- 3 tablespoons tandoori paste, unsweetened
- 1 teaspoon sea salt
- 1 block of tempeh (marinated and sliced into cubes)

Mix the yogurt and tandoori paste with the salt in a small glass bowl. Mix evenly and coat the tempeh cubes. Heat a skillet on medium and fry the tempeh until browned. Serve with salad or "riced" (grated) cauliflower or zucchini noodles.

Avocado and Tofu Bake

If you don't have time for breakfast, this is an option to prepare for lunch or late brunch. This recipe is simple. Scoop out the inside of an avocado, and stuff with the following ingredients:

- 2 tablespoons tofu scramble (recipe under breakfast) mixed with avocado
- 2 teaspoons dried or fresh dill or parsley
- Sliced green onions or chives for garnish

Combine ingredients inside the avocado shell and bake for 8-10 minutes. Serve with vegan keto toast or on its own.

Peanut Butter and Toast

This is a simple way to make your lunch if time is not available in the morning. The best bread to use is one with a thick texture and with lots of nuts and seeds. Peanut butter is a good source of protein, and it can be substituted with almond or hazelnut butter. Sprinkle cocoa powder as a topping.

Curried Broccoli and Kale Soup

This is a delicious lunch during a cold day that can be prepared the night before and reheated the next day. It is baked in the oven where all flavors combine and incorporate evenly. This meal combines two highly nutritious greens like broccoli and kale, with a curry flavor.

- 1 teaspoon garlic powder, plus 2 teaspoons
- 3 ½ cups grated or "riced" broccoli
- 3 tablespoons curry powder
- ½ teaspoon paprika
- 3 tablespoons olive oil
- 2 cups chopped kale; stems removed
- 1 teaspoon cumin powder or seeds
- 1 cup coconut milk
- 4 cups vegetable broth
- ¼ teaspoon sea salt
- 1 teaspoon black pepper
- Dash of salt or to taste

Combine and mix the broccoli, curry powder, olive oil, garlic powder, cumin, paprika, and salt in a medium mixing bowl. Spread the coated broccoli on a baking tray lined with baking paper, and roast them in the oven for 20 minutes. Remove, then set aside and prepare the soup. Chop the vegetables and measure the ingredients. Add the roasted broccoli mixture to the blender and mix. Prepare a large cooking pot where you add onion, oil, and 2 teaspoons garlic powder and sauté for 4-5 minutes. Add the vegetable broth and milk, vegetables, and broccoli "rice," along with the spices. Allow it to boil and then lower the heat, cooking on medium for 20 minutes. Garnish with parsley and bread and serve warm.

Sesame Tofu Bake

This is an easy, almost snack-like lunch that can be prepared in advance and made available for a quick, light meal.

- 2 teaspoons sesame oil
- ½ block extra firm tofu
- 1 cup vegetable broth
- 2 teaspoons sesame seeds

Slice the tofu into cubes. Pour the vegetable broth in a small or medium glass bowl and add sesame oil. Add the tofu to a resealable container and pour the broth and oil mixture over the cubes and marinate in the refrigerator overnight or for at least two hours. When ready to bake, warm the oven at 350 before preparing the other ingredients. Prepare a small baking pan with the drained tofu. Retain some of the liquid to pour over the tofu cubes, and sprinkle them with sesame seeds. Bake for 20 minutes until browned and serve.

Curried Cabbage

This is a fast and simple dish that requires little preparation, with the exception of slicing half of a head of cabbage, which can be done with a knife or shredder.

- 2 tablespoons tomato paste
- 2 tablespoons curry powder
- Half of a cabbage, sliced into thin leaves, stems removed
- 2-3 tablespoons olive oil

On medium-high heat, pour some oil in a skillet and add curry powder. Fry for one minute, then add the tomato paste. If the paste does not spread into the curry and oil, add an extra tablespoon. Add the cabbage slices and fry on medium heat until all of the cabbage has softened and is coated with the oil, curry, and tomato paste mix. Smoked tofu, fried onions, and mushrooms can be added to this dish.

Pizza Stuffed Peppers

If you have an extra green pepper or two, this recipe is a good way to make use of the pepper's shell, by stuffing and baking it as a "pizza."

- 2 green peppers, cut in half, seeds removed
- 2 cups vegan cheese
- 1 cup tomato sauce
- Optional spices: oregano, paprika, dill, parsley
- Sea salt and pepper
- Meat-free pepperoni (optional)
- Spinach

Fill each pepper with the following ingredients, in this order: a thin layer of tomato sauce, followed by vegan cheese, spinach, and meat-free pepperoni (one or two slices per green pepper "half"). Add salt and pepper on top and sprinkle with extra vegan cheese. Bake for 5-10 minutes in the oven. These can also be heated in the microwave.

Grilled "Cheese"

This recipe requires no major preparation, once you have your favorite vegan keto bread and vegan cheese chosen.

- One or two slices of vegan cheese
- Avocado, sliced (optional)
- 2-3 tablespoons olive oil
- Two slices of vegan keto bread

Warm a skillet with olive oil on medium heat. Add a thin layer of oil on one side of each bread slice, and add cheese, avocado, and other ingredients before forming the sandwich and frying on both sides until crispy and brown. Serve with a few slices of tomato or dill pickles or both.

Smoked Tofu and Arugula Salad

Smoked tofu can be found in the produce, meat-free area of your supermarket. It can also be prepared similarly to the sesame-baked tofu dish, only with liquid smoke in place of sesame oil. For convenience, smoked tofu can be purchased and is often available in several brands. Always choose the option with the least additives:

- ½ block of smoked tofu
- 1 lime squeezed
- 2 teaspoons olive oil
- Arugula, chopped

Pour some lime juice over the arugula in a mixing bowl and some olive oil and mix evenly. Toss and add a dash of sea salt (optional). Layer the smoked tofu over the arugula and serve.

Lettuce Wrap Sandwich

This is a sandwich or wrap option that eliminates bread altogether. To prepare a lettuce wrap, simply slice off large leaves of lettuce and form a taco-shaped wrap to fill with any of these ingredients:

- Vegan cheese slices
- Smoked tofu or another meat-free slice
- Pesto (dill, parsley or rosemary)
- Roasted eggplant
- Fried mushrooms
- Grilled portobello mushrooms

There are many more options to consider. Wrapping your lunch in lettuce is a way to add more fiber into your meals.

Tofu "Bacon," Fried Onions, and Avocado Sandwich

If you search in a few natural food stores, supermarkets, and, sometimes, local markets, you may find a soy-based bacon alternative. Smoked tofu is another option. This sandwich is full of flavor and can be reheated or toasted just before adding the ingredients. Fried onions can be caramelized by adding a low-carb sweetener, such as monk fruit in place of sugar. The avocado slices are added first, followed by the tofu bacon, then topped it with fried onions.

Fried Zucchini with "Cheese"

This recipe is as easy as slicing one or two zucchinis lengthwise and adding them to a heated skillet with olive oil. Fry on both sides for approximately 1-2 minutes on medium heat until slightly golden, then remove and serve with shredded vegan cheese.

Cream "Cheese" Bagel

The vegan keto breakfast bagel can work wonders in lunch options. A simple toasted bagel with vegan cream cheese is an easy way to enjoy lunch.

Vegan Deli Bagel

This bagel sandwich combines several sliced vegan "meat" and "cheese" flavors, along with other toppings, such as tomatoes, olive paste, avocado, and pickles. Hot peppers, salt, and black pepper are great options.

Spinach Guacamole Bagel

The guacamole recipe under "Snacks" is a great addition to any sandwich. Mixing the guacamole with raw or cooked spinach in between a bagel would provide more iron and minerals.

Smoked Tempeh, Mustard, and Arugula Bagel

Combining the sharp flavor of mustard, smoked tempeh (or tofu), and arugula is another option for using the breakfast bagel.

Spinach, Walnut, and Avocado Salad

If a light lunch suits your schedule best, this quickly put-together salad can keep you fed while you work or allow you to enjoy more of your lunch.

- 1 cup raw, washed spinach
- 1 tablespoon olive oil
- ½ cups crushed walnuts
- 1 ripe avocado
- 1 tablespoon lemon juice (or lime if you prefer)

In a small mixing bowl, place the lime or lemon juice with the olive oil, and set to the side to mix well. Place all the other ingredients in a large or medium bowl, then add the salad dressing and toss. Serve with soup, if available, or as a quick meal on its own.

Roasted Almonds and Walnuts on Arugula

Pan-roasted almonds and walnuts, with little or no olive oil, can be tossed with arugula for a simple, light salad. Combine 1 teaspoon balsamic vinegar, dried rosemary, and 1 teaspoon olive oil to create a dressing to add.

Stuffed Peppers and Wraps

These can be oven-baked, or if you're in a hurry, they can be heated in the microwave. Add baked tofu slices, curried tempeh, and any variety of finely chopped vegetables to use as stuffing for the peppers. They can also be an ideal wrap or taco for many other ingredients and recipe creations.

Dinners

Whether you need to replenish after a busy day, or you want to impress guests with a delicious dinner, there are plenty of options that fall under the vegan keto diet. These recipes will make a positive impact on anyone, even if they do not follow a plant-based and ketogenic diet.

Vegan Keto Moussaka

This dish is traditionally prepared with meat, which can be simply replaced or omitted in this recipe. Moussaka is a rich meal and also tasty comfort food. This is a simplified version of the recipe to adapt to the vegan keto diet:

- 1 cauliflower (ground or mashed into small pieces; riced cauliflower will work)
- 5 cloves of garlic (crushed)
- 1 eggplant slices into cubes
- Vegan cheese, shredded
- Sea salt (just a dash to taste)
- Vegan moussaka sauce (combine in a bowl and set aside):
    - 1 can tomato
    - 1 block of tempeh
    - 1 tablespoon onion powder
    - ¼ cup tomato paste
    - 1 tablespoon wine vinegar

o   Dash of salt and pepper

Grate the cauliflower (or use "riced" cauliflower) and cook until tender in a medium-sized pot with ¼ water. Drain and mash the cauliflower heads, add garlic, and set to the side. While preparing the cauliflower, the oven must be warmed to 350 degrees. Prepare the remaining ingredients. Line a baking dish with olive oil and begin to layer with the following: cauliflower mash as the first or bottom layer, followed by the next layer of vegan moussaka sauce. Continue to add layers of tempeh, eggplant slices, vegan cheese, and so on, ending with the top layer, which should be mashed cauliflower sprinkled with vegan cheese. Bake for 25-30 minutes and serve warm.

Zucchini "Zoodle" Pasta and Tomato Sauce

This is a twist on the simple spaghetti and tomato sauce dish, which is often served with meatballs as the main meal. It can also be served on the side if you want variety. In this recipe, the spaghetti noodles are replaced with zucchini noodles or "zoodles," which are prepared by spiral-slicing a raw zucchini into long spirals. Vegetable noodles are becoming popular and more readily available in grocery stores in the produce aisle. This meal is simple, with noodles and a tomato sauce, which can be the base for other toppings and ingredients.

- 3-4 cups spiral zucchini noodles, or two medium-sized zucchinis
- 2 tablespoons garlic powder
- 1 tablespoon oregano
- 2 cups of tomato sauce (unsweetened; if you use canned tomato sauce, check to confirm there are no added sugars or carbohydrates)
- 1 tcaspoon chili powder
- 2 teaspoons tomato paste
- ½ teaspoon sea salt
- 2 tablespoons dried basil

Prepare the zucchini noodles with a spiral slicer or use zoodles that were prepared ahead and add to a large colander. Rinse and set aside. Heat a medium cooking pot with tomato sauce and paste and stir in the spices, keeping the heat to low-medium for 10 minutes. This recipe will serve 3-4 portions. Add zucchini noodles to a small or medium plate and pour tomato sauce. Add shredded vegan cheese as a topping.

Vegan "meat" balls or soy-based ground "meat" can be added to the tomato sauce as it stews. When choosing a meat alternative, review the ingredients to rule out additives and sugars, which may be present in some brands. Pan-seared tempeh, prepared in a skillet, can be a great way to add protein to this pasta dish.

Broccoli and Cauliflower Fried Rice

"Riced" cauliflower is popular due to its mild flavor and consistency, which can replace rice in most dishes. Broccoli can also be a good replacement instead of cauliflower or combined together. To "rice" these vegetables, divide the head of cauliflower and broccoli into quarters or smaller for them to fit a food processor. You can also use a blender to grind and blend and them until they resemble a fine, rice-like texture and size. A grater can also be used in place of a food processor. The following ingredients, similar to regular fried rice, are also included:

- 1 teaspoon of garlic powder or finely ground fresh garlic
- Dash of pink Himalayan salt
- 1 small shallot or onion, finely and thinly chopped or grated
- 1 tablespoon olive, avocado, or coconut oil
- Dash of black pepper
- ¼ teaspoon of grated ginger root
- 1 teaspoon of sesame oil
- 4-5 tablespoons of chopped parsley or cilantro
- Slivered almonds

Warm a skillet on medium heat (or low heat) and add some oil of your choice. Add the riced cauliflower and broccoli, along with the garlic, to the pan and cook for 1-2 minutes, mixing occasionally. Add some salt and sesame oil and continue to fry for another 2 minutes, then add the grated ginger root. Cook for another 2 minutes or until the riced vegetables are mostly cooked but not mushy and still a bit crunchy. Serve and garnish with cilantro or parsley and slivered almonds.

This is a basic fried "rice" dish that can be served as a main meal with one of the following toppings:

- Fried mushrooms. Any variety, including shitake and portobello. Grilled portobello or regular mushrooms would make an excellent topping.
- Fried red onions
- Roasted almonds on the skillet. This can be prepared in advance and later added to the rice dish as a topping.
- Grilled eggplant

Portobello mushroom burgers

The strong, "meat-like" texture of portobello mushrooms make them an excellent substitute for meat or other vegetarian burger options. These burgers can be served with a vegan keto bun (or bread) on top of lettuce or on their own with toppings. During a summer barbeque, these are best grilled with other vegetables, including zucchini and eggplant. These burgers can be prepared on a barbeque grill or skillet:

- 2 portobello mushrooms
- ¼ cup balsamic vinegar
- 1 teaspoon dried basil
- Dash of salt and pepper
- 2 tablespoons olive oil
- 1 teaspoon dried oregano

Prepare the barbeque to grill portobello mushrooms by brushing with olive oil and preheat. Put the oil, pepper, balsamic vinegar, oregano, salt, and basil in a small mixing bowl and mix and set to the side. Grill for 5-6 minutes on each side, brushing the mushrooms with the marinade on both sides when switching.

If preparing in a skillet, heat on medium with olive oil and fry the mushrooms for 6-7 minutes on both sides, coating each side with the balsamic marinade. When the burgers are done, serve on a keto bun or a bed of fresh spinach sprinkled with fresh lime and balsamic dressing.

There are many topping options for portobello mushroom burgers:

- Skillet fried or raw sliced onions
- Sliced green pepper (fried or raw)
- Vegan cheese
- Smoked tofu (sliced and topped on the burgers)
- Lettuce (as a bun or topping)

Vegan Keto Lasagne

Lasagne can be easily switched from the high-carb original to a vegan keto version with a couple of simple changes: switching the noodles for cabbage and omit the meat (or add a vegan alternative). This is a meal that can vary considerably according to your favorite vegetables and flavors.

- 2 tablespoons olive oil
- One head of cabbage (medium)
- 2 zucchinis sliced thin, lengthwise
- 1 cup of spinach
- 2 cups of tomato sauce (plain, no additives)
- Vegan cream cheese
- 2 tablespoons shredded vegan cheese (cheddar or mozzarella)

Before any preparations, warm up the oven to 350 degrees. Wash the vegetables with running water and cut them up. Evenly coat with some olive oil a large baking pan and spread a thin layer of tomato sauce. Add cabbage leave slices over the tomato sauce layer, and make sure all of the stems are removed before doing so. Ensure the cabbage covers the pan evenly, and add another layer of vegan cream cheese, then spinach, tomato sauce, another layer of cabbage, then more cheese, tomato sauce, zucchini, and continue to layer until either cabbage or zucchini is the top layer.

Sprinkle lightly with olive oil and cover in shredded vegan cheese. Bake for 40 minutes and serve warm.

Other ingredients to add include vegan ground "meat," which can be added as a layer. Vegan shredded cheese is another option.

The Ultimate Vegan Keto Platter

This is an ideal dinner idea for an event or when you expect guests. All of the following ingredients are arranged on a large, oval-sized serving platter:

- Dill pickles, sliced lengthwise
- Fried mushrooms
- Smoked or pan-seared tofu (in cubes or slices)
- Cauliflower and broccoli (cut into small florets)
- Vegan cheese slices
- Black olives
- Grilled zucchini (or fried for 5-6 minutes on a skillet)
- Fresh berries
- Dried coconut pieces
- Celery sticks

Cauliflower "Macaroni and Cheese"

The original macaroni and cheese dish can be adjusted to the vegan keto version by substituting the macaroni for cauliflower and adding vegan cheese. For this recipe, add more than one type or flavor of vegan cheese to increase the variety and strength of taste for this dish.

- 1 head of cauliflower
- 1 teaspoon of paprika
- 2 cups shredded vegan cheese (cheddar flavor)
- ½ cup almond flour
- ½ cup vegan dried or "parmesan" cheese
- ¼ cup olive oil
- 1 cup shredded vegan cheese (mozzarella flavor)

Warm up the oven on 350-degree temperature while you prepare everything else. Slice the head of cauliflower into small pieces, approximately ½ to 1-inch in size. Using some olive oil, grease a medium-sized rectangular baking pan and add half of the cauliflower. Combine the cheddar and mozzarella-flavored vegan cheeses and blend in a medium mixing bowl, then add a layer of half of the cauliflower over the bottom layer. Add the remaining cauliflower to the cheese mix and combine and add to the rest of the pan. In a second small bowl, mix the dried vegan cheese and almond flour. Coat the top of the casserole with the dry mix. Sprinkle with paprika. Bake for not more than half an hour. By then, the top should be golden, but it would be better to check every 10 minutes. Serve warm.

Vegan Keto Chili

Skipping the meat, cheese, and beans in a pot of chili may seem like a change to a completely different dish altogether, though there are some great options for preparing a healthy chili that is both low in carbs and free of animal products. Chilis are best cooked slowly. When you have time to stew, add and stir ingredients for two hours. In a large cooking pot, add 4-6 cans of diced tomatoes on low to medium heat, along with any spices you wish to add (salt, pepper, chili pepper or flakes, oregano, paprika, etc.). The following ingredients may be considered:

- Chopped celery
- Spinach
- Chopped onions
- Crush garlic
- Diced green peppers
- Vegan ground "beef"
- Okra, chopped
- Jalapeno peppers
- Mushrooms
- Zucchini

Once the chili is ready to be served, garnish with vegan cheese.

Vegan Keto Bruschetta Bread

This recipe is best prepared with a natural-tasting vegan keto bread. It is very similar to regular bruschetta using the following ingredients:

- 6-8 slices of bread
- 2-3 tablespoons olive oil
- 3 tomatoes
- 1 small onion, finely chopped
- ½ cup of freshly chopped basil leaves
- 2 teaspoons balsamic vinegar
- 1 clove of crushed garlic.
- Salt and pepper.

Before preparing the ingredients, heat the oven to 350 degrees and then line with parchment paper a baking tray. Add the bread to the tray and coat them lightly in olive oil. Warm the bread until toasted (about 10 minutes) and transfer on another tray to cool. Combine and mix well the rest of the ingredients in a bowl. Coat each slice of bread with these toppings and serve. This bruschetta recipe goes well with chili and soups.

Roasted Butternut Squash

This is a simple recipe that can fulfill a meal with a tasty, mouth-watering vegetable. It's a dish that's best enjoyed at home, as it is prepared in the oven and enjoyed as soon as it's ready:

- 1 medium butternut squash (if not available, another squash variety will work)
- Salt
- Olive oil

Warm the oven to 350 degrees before preparing the squash. Line a baking sheet with paper suitable for baking. Rinse butternut squash with cool water and slice in half. Lightly coat both halves in oil and sprinkle with salt. Bake for approximately half an hour and enjoy.

Butternut Squash Soup

If you are in the mood for soup, use the recipe for roasted squash using the following:.

- 3 tablespoons olive oil
- Roasted butternut squash, peeled and chopped into smaller pieces
- Dash of salt
- 1 celery stalk, thinly sliced
- 1 teaspoon black pepper
- Thyme
- 1 small onion, grated or thinly sliced
- 3-4 cups vegetable broth

Place all the ingredients into a medium cooking pot on medium-high heat. Wait for it to boil before removing from the heat to cool. Transfer the contents to a food processor, blending in batches, if needed, until smooth. Return soup to the pot and reheat until ready to serve. Garnish with thyme.

Curried Pumpkin Soup

This soup is created similarly to butternut squash, replacing the squash with pumpkin puree and adding curry powder and coconut milk.

- 3 tablespoons olive oil
- 2 cups pumpkin puree
- 1 teaspoon black pepper
- 1 celery stalk, thinly sliced
- 2-3 tablespoons curry powder
- ½ cup coconut milk
- 1 small onion, grated or thinly sliced
- Dash of salt
- 3-4 cups vegetable broth

Combine all ingredients into a large cooking pot and allow to boil under a medium-high flame. Just after boiling, remove from heat. Transfer to a food processor when cool and blend. You might need to do it in batches until the soup is smooth or according to desired consistency. Return the soup to the pot and reheat until ready to serve.

Cream of Asparagus Soup

This is a delicious soup that pairs well with salad, bread, or a baked vegetable. It can be a side dish or a main meal.

- 2 tablespoons olive oil
- 2 lbs of asparagus, chopped into small, bite-sized pieces
- Sea salt
- Black pepper
- 3-4 cups vegetable broth
- 1 clove of garlic, minced
- ½ cup almond or coconut milk
- Chives and dill for garnish

Prepare and warm a large saucepan or pot. Add the olive oil under medium flame and add garlic. Cook for 1-2 minutes and then add the asparagus, pepper, and salt. Continue to cook and add the broth when the asparagus is tender. Simmer the broth for another 10 minutes, then remove from the heat to cool. Move to the blender and process in batches until all is done. Return to the pot to reheat. Serve with dill or chives as a garnish.

Cream of Cauliflower Soup

The same delicious and creamy soup can be adapted for cauliflower.

- 2 tablespoons olive oil
- 1 head of cauliflower, chopped into small, bite-sized pieces
- Sea salt
- Black pepper
- 3-4 cups vegetable broth
- 1 diced onion
- ½ cup almond or coconut milk
- Paprika

Set a large cooking pot over a medium flame on the stove. When warmed, add some olive oil, followed by the garlic, and cook it for 1-2 minutes. Add the cauliflower, pepper, salt and continue to cook until the cauliflower is soft. Add the broth and simmer for about ten more minutes. When cooked to your preference, remove from the heat to cool. Move to the blender and process in batches, when needed, and return to the pot to reheat. Serve and garnish with paprika.

Skillet Meals for Dinner: The Easy Way to Vegan Keto

There are many options for stir fry dishes that can fit into any lifestyle or way of eating, including a plant-based ketogenic diet.

The following recipes are various skillet meal combinations that can be served on their own, with zucchini noodles, or "riced" broccoli or cauliflower. All skillet meals are prepared using olive oil:

Skillet Meal 1: Tofu, Spinach and Garlic

This is a simple but effective way to get a lot of nutrients and good boost to your immune system without many ingredients. Once the skillet is heated, add the tofu first, followed by garlic then spinach. Mushrooms can be added at the end if desired.

Skillet Meal 2: Tempeh, Cabbage, and Onions

Tempeh is a powerful source of nutrients, including B12. Cabbage and onions make a good fit, as they are both strong in flavor and enhance the dish.

Skillet Meal 3: Cauliflower, Garlic, Ginger, and Green Beans

Before you begin, crush the garlic and ginger and sauté lightly, then add the green beans and cauliflower.

Skillet Meal 4: Asparagus, Garlic, and Mushrooms

Any variety of mushroom will work well with this dish. Always add mushrooms last, as they cook faster than the other vegetables. Add sesame seeds for extra flavor.

Skillet Meal 5: Bell Peppers, Okra, and Eggplant

Add extra salt to soften the eggplant, and add okra last, as it cooks faster than the other ingredients.

Skillet Meal 6: Artichoke, Spinach, and Mushrooms

Artichoke and spinach work well in dips and sauces, and their flavors also complement one another in this skillet. Mushrooms are another good way to enhance the overall taste of this dish.

Skillet Meal 7: Brussel Sprouts, Vegan Butter, and Garlic

These powerfully nutritious vegetables can stand on their own with some garlic and butter or combined with other vegetables. They are delicious as an oven-roasted dish sprinkled with vegan cheese and sea salt.

Skillet Meal 8: Asparagus, Almonds, and Garlic

Garlic is consistently a good option for skillet meals and a good way to boost your immune health. Almonds can be slightly toasted and slivered before adding to this meal. Top with vegan cheese.

Skillet Meal 9: Celery, Green Beans, and Almonds

This is simply pan-seared green beans added to celery and roasted almonds.

Skillet Meal 10: Baked Sesame Tofu, Snow Peas, and Garlic

This prepared tofu can be sliced and fried with garlic and snow peas.

Skillet Meal 11: Bok Choy, Broccoli, and Garlic

This combination works best with some soy sauce added, though this is optional. Garlic and olive oil will bring out the flavors in these vegetables as well.

All skillet meal ideas are guides only and can be simply combined or changed according to individual taste and preference.

Desserts

Chocolate Avocado Mousse

This dessert requires only three ingredients and can be made within 1-2 minutes. If you have a craving to satisfy, or you simply want to create a simple and easy dessert on short notice, this is the perfect option.

- One very ripe, large avocado
- 2 tablespoons dark, unsweetened cocoa or dark chocolate powder (melted dark chocolate also works in this recipe)

Combine the avocado and cocoa in a small mixing bowl. Mash the avocado, incorporating the cocoa powder until smooth and blended. Serve immediately in a small dessert bowl (makes 1-2 servings). Add a topping, such as whipped coconut cream that is sweetened with stevia or monk fruit.

Cinnamon and Almond Cookies

This is a good option for comfort food, especially when you are craving something sugary or high in carbs. These cookies are baked in the oven and only require five ingredients:

- 2 cups of almond flour
- ¼ cup low-carb sweetener (stevia or monk fruit)
- 2 tablespoons of chia seeds
- 2 tablespoons cinnamon powder
- 3-4 tablespoons freshly squeezed orange

To start, warm up the oven to 350 degrees. Grind the chia seeds to smaller pieces using a food processor. Add the sweetener to incorporate well with the chia seeds. Add to a medium bowl with the remaining ingredients and mix everything together. A thick dough will form, which should provide enough for 7-8 small cookies. Roll into small half-inch balls and put on a paper-lined baking sheet. You can create other shapes, or you can simply make balls that you can flatten with a spoon or fork. Bake for 14-15 minutes.

Fat Bombs: A New Way to Treat Yourself on the Vegan Keto Diet

Fat bombs are healthy fat fuel treats that can be prepared quickly and with only a few ingredients. They are usually stored in the freezer or refrigerator and reserved for when you need that sweet fix or treat. Once you try a few fat bomb recipes, you'll want to experiment with more ingredients, flavors, and ideas for new combinations. Before you begin, you'll need a few items to get started:

- Small-sized muffin tray
- Reusable liners (single-use paper liners can be used, though reusable is recommended)
- Ice cube tray

Chocolate Peanut Butter Cups Fat Bombs

If you love chocolate and peanut butter together, this is a win-win recipe. It only requires three ingredients:

- 1 cup of peanut butter (unsweetened)
- 1 cup melted dark, unsweetened chocolate or cocoa
- 2-3 tablespoons monk fruit or stevia

When melting the chocolate, add the monk fruit or stevia and stir in thoroughly. Half of the melted chocolate will be used for the bottom layer and the remainder for the top, with the peanut butter in the center. Prepare a muffin tray (small size is ideal, any size will work), and add one layer of melted chocolate to the bottom of each liner, up to one third, then store for 20 minutes in a chiller or freezer. When ready, add the second layer (peanut butter) for another third of each cup, then return to the freezer. After another 20 minutes, add the final layer of chocolate, and freeze it again for another 20 minutes. The cups are now ready to enjoy. They should either remain in the freezer or can be kept in the refrigerator until eaten, as they will melt quickly at room temperature.

Coconut Fat Bombs

These treats are one of the best ways to increase healthy fat in your vegan keto diet. All of the ingredients are coconut-based. MCT oil can be added with the coconut oil (an extra teaspoon) to increase the fat amount further.

- ¼ cup coconut butter
- ¼ cup coconut oil (or 1/8 coconut oil and 1/8 MCT oil)
- 2 tablespoons shredded coconut, unsweetened
- 1 teaspoon monk fruit or stevia

Combine all the items on the list in a glass bowl, and mix everything until the sweetener is completely dissolved and incorporated with the other ingredients. Scoop the blend into an ice cube tray or small silicone molds and freeze or refrigerate for 10-15 minutes.

Strawberry "Cheesecake" Fat Bombs

These are tasty bite-sized strawberry cheesecake fat bombs made with vegan cream cheese and fresh or frozen strawberries:

- ¼ cup coconut butter (peanut or almond butter)
- ¼ cup vegan cream cheese
- 2-3 tablespoons coconut oil
- 3 tablespoons low-carb sweetener
- ½ cup sliced strawberries

Combine the ingredients in a small bowl and mix well. Scoop into silicone moulds or a muffin tray and freeze for approximately 20 minutes, then enjoy.

Pistachio Fat Bombs

- 2/3 tablespoons coconut oil
- ¼ cup pistachios (ground)
- 1-2 tablespoons low-carb sweetener

Combine and mix ingredients in a small bowl, making sure all of the ground pistachios are blended into the coconut oil and sweetener evenly. Scoop into silicone molds or a muffin tray and freeze for 15-20 minutes.

Almond Fat Bombs

- 2-3 tablespoons coconut oil
- ¼ cup almond butter
- 1-2 tablespoons ground almonds
- 1-2 tablespoons low-carb sweetener

Mix all of the ingredients in a glass bowl and transfer to a muffin tray or silicone molds. Ground almonds can be omitted or substituted with slivered almonds or almond meal if desired. Freeze for 20 minutes before consuming.

Chocolate Fat Bombs

If you simply love chocolate, these are a delicious option for a quick snack.

- ¼ cup coconut butter
- ¼ cup cocoa powder or melted dark, unsweetened chocolate
- 2 teaspoons coconut oil
- 1-2 tablespoons low-carb sweetener

Combine ingredients and mix well. If you are using melted chocolate instead of cocoa powder, heat a small pan on low heat and melt chocolate until it is even without any lumps before mixing. Both cocoa powder and melted chocolate can be used together in this recipe, for a double-chocolate effect. Shredded coconut is another option if you enjoy coconut and cocoa combined.

Pumpkin Fat Bombs

When pumpkins are in season, use this recipe as an easy way to use up any leftover fresh pumpkin, or you use the canned version.

- 1 teaspoon cinnamon
- 2 tablespoons pumpkin puree
- 2 teaspoons coconut oil
- 1-2 tablespoons low-carb sweetener
- 1 teaspoon nutmeg
- ¼ cup coconut butter

In a mixing bowl, medium in size, combine and mix well all ingredients on the list. Add an extra tablespoon of pumpkin puree, and increase cinnamon and nutmeg spices if desired. Pour mixture into silicone molds or a tray and freeze for at least20 minutes.

Cardamom-Cinnamon Fat Bombs

A unique and tasty option for fat bombs, the combination of both cinnamon and cardamom create a delicious treat. If you prefer one spice more than the other, simply remove one and double the preference:

- 2 tablespoons coconut oil
- ½ teaspoon cinnamon
- ½ teaspoon cardamom
- ½ teaspoon low-carb sweetener (optional)
- ½ teaspoon vanilla extract
- ¼ cup finely shredded coconut

Combine and thoroughly mix all the ingredients in a small bowl and place on a muffin tray or silicone molds to freeze for at least 15-20 minutes.

Vegan Keto Brownies

Brownies are a great dessert and snack at the same time. The ingredients in brownies can be changed to suit a variety of flavor and dietary options. The key to successful brownies is keeping them moist and soft:

- ½ coconut butter
- 6 tablespoons low-carb sweetener
- 2 teaspoons flaxseeds combined with 4 teaspoons warm water (in a small bowl)
- 1 teaspoon baking powder
- 1 teaspoon vanilla
- 1 cup almond flour
- ¾ cups cocoa powder
- ¼ cup ground walnuts or almonds

Preheat oven to 350 degrees. Combine all of the ingredients in a large bowl and blend thoroughly, making sure there are no lumps. Prepare a square or rectangular baking dish. Grease with olive oil and add the batter, spreading it evenly across the pan. Bake for 15 minutes.

Cheesecake Cup

This recipe is prepared raw, with no baking or cooking required. All that is needed is a tall glass and the following items layered from bottom to top:

- 2 tablespoons almond flour mixed with 1 teaspoon low-carb sweetener
- 1 cup vegan cream cheese, blended with monk fruit and 1 teaspoon of coconut milk
- Add fresh fruit, cinnamon, or cocoa powder on top of the cup
- 1 teaspoon vanilla extract (added to cream cheese and sweetener)

Pumpkin Cheesecake Cup

Apply the same recipe used for regular cheesecake cups. This recipe varies from the previous one when you combine ¼ cup of pumpkin puree with the vegan cream cheese. This cup can be garnished with nutmeg and cinnamon.

Cocoa Cheesecake Cup

Replace the ¼ pumpkin puree with the same portion of cocoa powder or melted dark, unsweetened chocolate. The topping can be cocoa powder, cinnamon, or a combination of both.

Lemon-Lime Cheesecake Cup

Add 1 tablespoon of lime juice and 1 of lemon juice into a small bowl and combine, then add to the regular cheesecake cup recipe.

Fruit Salad

Keto-friendly fruits tend to be few, though there is a good combination of low-carb fruits that can be enjoyed in small doses. These fruits can be added "as is" or chopped into smaller, easy-to-eat sizes for one serving:

- Kiwi
- Strawberries
- Lime and lemon juice (combined, 1 tablespoon)
- Firm and slightly ripe avocado slices

Dark Chocolate and Berries

Some dark, unsweetened or similar low-carb chocolate options are a great fit for the vegan keto diet. One bar of this specialty treat can be expensive, though only a small amount is needed to melt and pour over berries or other desserts like crepe or ice cream. Dark chocolate, when melted, can be an excellent dip for fruits.

Vegan Keto Ice Cream — Cocoa and Vanilla

This is a one-serving ice cream recipe that combines the following few ingredients.

- 1 tablespoon cocoa powder
- 2 tablespoons monk fruit
- 1 teaspoon vanilla extract
- 1 cup coconut milk

Combine and mix all the ice cream ingredients in a glass mixing bowl, and pour the contents to a jar or wide container and freeze.

Vegan Keto Ice Cream — Cinnamon

Combine all the ingredients from the above recipe, and substitute cocoa powder for cinnamon. Cardamom may be used in addition to cinnamon or as a replacement.

Drinks

Cardamom and Ginger Spice Tea Drink

This is a delicious, warm drink that can be enjoyed during cold weather or as a late-night treat before bed. The base can be water, green tea, or coconut milk

- 2 cups of coconut or almond milk (or water with green tea)
- 2 tablespoons dried ginger root
- 2 tablespoons crushed cardamom pods
- 2 tablespoons low-carb sweetener

Add and mix all the ingredients to a small cooking saucepan and bring to a boil on low heat, while stirring in the spices and sweetener. Once it is ready, serve it warm with a cinnamon stick.

Matcha Green Tea Latte

Matcha green tea is a delicious tea that is full of antioxidants. It can simply be prepared by steeping green tea powder or leaves in a cup of hot water to serve with or without sweetener.

A latte is prepared using milk, and in this drink, either almond or coconut milk can be used as a base. If you don't have a latte or espresso machine, this drink can be prepared on a stovetop by boiling the milk and adding the following:

- 2 tablespoons matcha green tea powder
- 2 cups coconut or almond milk
- 2 tablespoons low-carb sweetener

Bring all ingredients to a boil on low to medium heat and serve in a mug.

Regular Coffee With Almond Milk and Sweetener

If you are a coffee drinker and enjoy this way of getting your caffeine fix, simply brew your favorite blend of coffee and add almond milk and your favorite low-carb sweetener, similar to adding cream and sugar, only without the dairy and carbs! Coconut milk is another option, though almond milk tends to mix better with coffee.

Iced MCT Coffee

MCT oil or coconut oil can be added to a hot cup of coffee or any other beverage to increase the amount of healthy fats in your diet. Iced coffee is an easy way to get a dose of MCT oil while spicing up the drink with cinnamon, low-carb sweetener or cocoa powder. One or two teaspoons of MCT oil or coconut oil is all that's needed. Almond milk can also be added, along with ice, and blended for a tasty treat.

Cucumber and Lime Water

Water infused with natural flavor is a great way to quench your thirst during the warmer months or a vigorous workout at the gym. All that is needed is a large jug of filtered or spring water, one lime cut into quarters, and 5-6 slices of cucumber. Chill overnight or for several hours to flavor the water and serve with ice.

Lemon and Mint Water

Like the cucumber and lime water drink, this flavor option is the same, only with fresh mint leaves and lemon. Lime can be substituted for lemon if desired.

Vegan Keto Eggnog

A holiday favorite, eggnog is usually very high in sugar and dairy, though it is a drink many people look forward to during the festive season. In this recipe, the dairy is replaced with coconut milk, which is thick and tasty for this beverage. Maple or vanilla flavoring can be added, though this is optional:

- 2 cups coconut milk
- ¼ cups water
- 2 tablespoons vanilla or maple flavor
- ½ teaspoon nutmeg
- ½ teaspoon cinnamon
- ½ cup raw almonds or cashews

Soak the almonds or cashews overnight in ¼ cup of water so they become tender. If you want to create this drink in a shorter time frame, the minimum soaking time is one hour. When the almonds or cashews are ready, combine with the rest of the ingredients in a blender and mix for one minute. Serve chilled.

Berry juice

If you have a juicer, a blend of berries combined with water is a cool, refreshing treat in the summer. This recipe is easy to create with a handful of fresh berries (about 1 cup) and 1-2 cups of water. Add to a blender and mix until all of the berries are blended well. Add ice cubes and serve.

Chapter 8: Bonus Chapter: Enjoying the Vegan Keto Diet and Recipes Without Expensive Ingredients

How do you save money and budget on the vegan keto diet? Food is often expensive, and with so many options and places to choose from, sticking with a budget is difficult. Balancing the grocery budget only becomes more challenging with a new diet. As with any way of eating, there are ways to reduce and control spending to get the most out of your money while sticking with a healthy vegan keto diet:

- Prepare a list of basic goods that you need every week, and "build" or add more food items according to your expenses for food. Allow some extra funds for extra items or unexpected increase in some items.

- Buy in bulk. This is especially a good idea for snacks and baking ingredients. Avoid the higher costs of goods from packaging and buying more of one item than you want or need. Choose 2-3 recipes and note the measured amounts of each ingredient to use as a guide for the purchase. For example, if you only require a ½ cup of almond flour, buy 1-2 cups in bulk instead of purchasing a full package, unless you have a lot of baking planned. For large volume baking and cooking, buying in bulk may or may not be advantageous, depending on the types of items you need. Research ahead and compare prices whenever possible.

- Keep it simple. The most expensive foods are often processed or packaged and not the healthiest option. These types of foods are usually chosen for snacks. Even protein bars, low-carb pastries, and other goods claim to be ketogenic and vegan, but they are usually overpriced and may contain hidden sugars and other ingredients that can hinder your progress. There are plenty of easy recipes for homemade versions that can be prepared, many without baking or too many ingredients. You can also get these at a fraction of the cost.
- Choose whole foods. Ditch the packaged kale chips for fresh kale, and make your own snack. Scoop a handful of raw almonds instead of potato chips. Find a fresh, natural alternative for snacking to replace old habits. This may take time, although it will be healthier and cheaper overall.

Chapter 9: Vegan Keto Diet for Long-Term Success in Health and Weight Loss Goals

Succeeding at the vegan keto diet is all up to how well you can adapt and follow new food choices, learn about nutrients, and avoid processed and high-carb foods. Making notes, researching new products, learning about the different vegetables and fruits (both local and imported) are part of a new approach to diet. Such a diet does not focus on the restrictions but on the opportunities of trying many new foods. The information in this book provides a foundation and guide to start you on the right path to achieving a sustainable and long-term diet plan that will result in a better way of living and eating for life.

Conclusion

Thank you for making it to the end of *Vegan Keto Diet: The Ultimate Ketogenic Diet and Cookbook, With Low-Carb and Vegan Keto Bread Recipes to Maximize Weight Loss and Special Ideas to Build Your Keto Vegan Meal Plan.*

Let us hope it was informative and able to provide you all of the tools you need to achieve your goals, whatever they may be.

The next step is to work on your diet and take action!

Finally, if you found this book useful in any way, a review on Amazon is always appreciated!

Printed in Great Britain
by Amazon

32558495R00108